Castles in Britain

Castles in Britain

an illustrated guide

by

Stuart Barton

First Published June 1973
Second Impression May 1974

Text by Stuart Barton
Art Editor Richard Munday
Head of Research Mary Hayman
Picture Editor Martin Miller
Edited by Tony Curtis
Original material supplied by T.M. Andrews, B.A.

Acknowledgements

Suzanne Coles
Michael Gorton Design
Julia Reeves
Kelly Murphy

A. F. Adams, Shawbury   Bellinghams, Brampton   G. Berry, Kendal   R. Booker, Worcester
F. Cooper, Kenilworth   Courier Printing and Publishing Co. Ltd., Tunbridge Wells
Cumberland Newspapers Ltd., Carlisle   East Anglia Daily Times, Ipswich   Eastern County
Newspapers Ltd., Norwich   Essex Chronicle, Chelmsford   Essex County Newspapers
Ltd., Colchester   Harry Green, Weymouth   J. A. Hartup, Lancaster   Hertfordshire
Mercury, Hertford   Kent Messenger, Maidstone   Kintore School, Kintore   R. Knight,
Southampton   Leicester Mercury, Leicester   Philipson Studios, Newcastle upon Tyne
J. Rowe, Orford   Salisbury Times, Salisbury   Shah Studio, Penzance   Turners Photo-
graphy Ltd., Newcastle upon Tyne. A special thanks to Librarians throughout Great
Britain, without whose kind help this book would not have been possible.

PREFACE

The British countryside abounds with castles of many types and sizes in all states of preservation or decay. Almost every area has its castle from which, at some time, it has been ruled for better or worse and, often, plunged into bloody conflict. Indeed, the histories of all castles are the histories both of the areas in which they stand and of their Lords — the powerful nobles whose deeds created much of the history of the British nation.

It is, perhaps, something of this which accounts for the curiously deep-seated fascination which castles — even the most ruinous of them — hold for people of all walks of life, causing queues to form outside admission gates before they open on summer mornings and causing attendance figures to show a steady annual increase.

Fortunately, a large number of British castles are in the capable hands of the Department of the Environment and the National Trust, both of which organisations expend a considerable amount of energy and money to ensure that the monuments in their care are kept in good condition for the safe enjoyment of visitors. Each organisation, too, publishes lists of properties it administers and each produces, for individual sites, guide books which manage to be extremely informative without recourse to pedantry.

Apart from the work done by these two organisations, we have reason to be grateful to the many individuals and societies who, over the years, have worked to preserve castles across the country. A considerable number of castles have fallen into the hands of local authorities, however, and it is sad to see how many of these have been treated. It would seem that the normal council reaction to a castle has been to convert it into an office or to conceal it behind a miscellany of municipal shrubbery. Some few councils seem unable to rise even to these heights and the castles in their care find themselves fenced off and left to fill slowly with refuse until the day they can be pulled down as safety hazards and their sites used to more profitable ends.

By and large, however, the Castles of Britain, many of which have stood for some eight hundred years, seem likely to survive for a good many more.

The primary purpose of this collection is to list, illustrate and locate as many castles as possible for the benefit of the many who enjoy visiting historic sites. No great attempt has been made to give scholarly descriptions of the buildings or their histories since sources abound in plenty for these purposes, rather, the intention is to offer, in a single volume, references to over three hundred castles of Britain which, it is hoped, will be of interest and use to sightseer and student alike.

Stuart Barton

Printed and Bound in Great Britain by
T. & A. Constable Ltd., Hopetoun Street, Edinburgh

CONTENTS

ENGLAND

SCOTLAND

WALES

THE DEVELOPMENT OF THE CASTLE

There are hundreds of castles in Britain, yet only comparatively few are generally well known and the great majority pass unrecognised, perhaps even by the people who live closest to them. This is hardly surprising since many of these were built in the earliest part of the Middle Ages, principally of earth, and their superficial remains are grassy hillocks scattered over the countryside. William of Normandy (William I) and his followers introduced these first castles to Britain and they were one of the principal tools both in his successful invasion of the land and the Norman Kings' subsequent domination of it. They had great advantages for the invaders, being quick to erect using locally obtained materials. Their chief parts were a tall mound with a flat top, called a Motte and a lower enclosure, the Bailey, which covered a much larger area. Often there was more than one Bailey but nearly always one Motte only was constructed. Where they could make use of natural features the Normans did so but otherwise both parts of the castle were put up from scratch using manual labour. The Bayeux Tapestry,

made about 20 years after the invasion of 1066, shows the Motte at Hastings being built like this. A ditch surrounded the whole castle, separating the Motte and Bailey and forming a figure of eight so that a wooden trestle bridge, or a steep flight of steps cut in the mound, had to be used for communication between the two. In addition a wooden palisade ran round the top of both parts of the castle and a sturdy wooden tower of one or more storeys rose from the centre of the Motte. It is clear that the Motte was the strong point of the castle but it also served as a residence for the lord and his administrative headquarters and a watchtower too. Contemporary manuscripts describe towers as tall as three storeys and also indicate that the palisade of the Bailey was defended by wooden towers along the circuit, though this practice must have been rather rare, and excavation has revealed that a second line of posts behind the first providing support for a wall walk was more common.

William did not build all the castles of the Conquest by himself but relied on the efforts of his followers who were given

parcels of land in return for their war service. The site chosen for the castle was always of prime importance and the Norman Lords were ruthless in establishing it, tearing down existing buildings and dwelling houses if necessary and very often the Lord himself, or the constable appointed by him as commander, supervised its construction using local labour (often forced). Towns on trade routes across the country, crossing points or fords of rivers or their highest navigable points, the tops of strategic valleys or mountain passes, all these were places where castles became established and when dominance over a locality was complete some castles used in the initial conquest were probably abandoned. William and his successors were careful to grant the most valuable parts of the country to their nearest kinsmen who they could trust to secure those parts against invasion by the King's enemies, mainly the French and the Danes. This trust was sometimes disastrously misplaced but nevertheless the simple Motte and Bailey castle came to be a common part of the British landscape, as it still is for those with the knowledge to spot it.

Shell Keep

Motte and Bailey

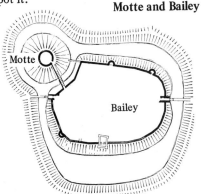

The arrangement of the defences in the first castles was simple but extremely effective, for the Tower on the Motte, or Keep as it came to be called, was able to command the open spaces of the Bailey whilst its position as a separate unit gave its occupants the option of escape if the situation required it — a part of the Bayeux Tapestry depicting an attack on the Motte at Dol shows Duke Conan doing just this.

It is not surprising therefore, that when permanent stone castles came to be built they often followed exactly the layout of the original earthworks. Some castles like London and Colchester were built in stone from the beginning but, more often, certain parts only of existing sites were converted, usually starting with the Bailey Gateway and the Keep. Because earth takes a long time to settle before it becomes suitable as a base for heavy masonry, builders often dispensed with the Mottes and constructed tall square towers in lieu. Sometimes however, the wooden palisades on them came to be replaced exactly by stone, these constructions being called Shell Keeps. The name is obvious, since several were constructed and remain to this day, like shells, just strong circular walls. Wooden buildings leant against the inside of the wall but in some instances, as at Restormel, the interior comprised commodious permanent stone buildings.

A stone gatehouse to the Bailey often came before the Keep in precedence since its entrance bore the brunt of an attack, being comparatively the weakest part of the castle. A simple square tower was built, having a passage through the centre, defended perhaps by a drawbridge and portcullis facing the field and stout wooden doors at the inside end. The portcullis was a criss-cross timber gate strengthened with iron (many are still in existence) and raised or lowered in grooves cut in the sides of the passage. Its lifting machinery occupied a chamber above. The drawbridge was hinged on the front of the tower and spanned the Bailey ditch. It could be drawn up by muscle power turning a windlass or helped by counterweights. In later years, more elaborate mechanisms operated both the portcullis and drawbridge. Some gate-houses had a turning bridge. This was pivoted like a see-saw at the front of the gatehouse but as it turned, the back part, swinging into a pit provided for it, left a gaping void as an additional obstacle in the way of attackers. It also counterbalanced the front end so that less effort was required to raise it.

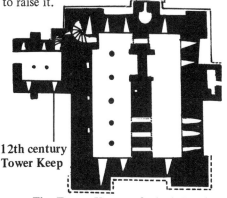

12th century
Tower Keep

The Tower Keeps, of which London, Colchester and Rochester are early examples, are of a type that became generally built in the reign of Henry II, who succeeded Stephen in 1135. Though Henry I (William the Conqueror's youngest son) built stone castles, many wood and earth examples probably came into being during the anarchy of Stephen's reign (caused by the bid for power of Matilda, Henry's daughter, eventually terminated by agreement at Wallingford). Henry II, her son, forbade the building of castles except by Royal Licence. Many were constructed with this permission during his reign and he was a vigorous builder himself. His Keeps are tall, plain buildings, square on plan, with walls of great thickness and a strong cross wall inside for extra rigidity. This also gave the defenders extra cover if their assailants finally broke in. The entrance door was above ground floor level, reached by a staircase contained in a well-fortified fore-

building which, in itself, was often provided with a drawbridge and portcullis. The only openings in the Keep walls were slits for bowmen, chutes for the soil of garde-robes (the lavatories of the time) and some windows in the upper storeys. These were usually reached by a narrow, winding stair located in the thickness of the wall in one corner. Thin buttresses and solid plinths at the base were usually the sole features relieving the plainness of the walls outside, except for crenellations (tooth-like formations) at the wall head. These gave cover to defenders, who stood on the parapet behind, enabling them to dodge the missiles of their assailants. The floors and roofs of the Keeps were of wood, the latter being steeply pitched, and the holes for the beams supporting them can be seen inside the many ruined Keeps in Britain.

Let us consider some of the main reasons for the new developments in castle design.

To begin with, apart from its durability, stone was used because of its resistance to current methods of attack; fire and direct assault over the walls being most common. A stone wall could be built higher without sacrificing too much strength and it was fireproof. However, European nobles learnt fresh techniques of attack and defence during their campaigns in the nine crusades (1097–1272) where massive stone throwing engines and other siege equipment were operated against powerful stone fortresses designed to resist them. One of the chief drawbacks of the plain stone wall with its crenellations was that it exposed a soldier to the besiegers as he defended it. For this reason, many castles also acquired a removable enclosed timber gallery, or hoarding, running around the outside of the wall head, which allowed protected observation and defence of the base of the wall as well as to the front. Wooden beams supporting this gallery were inserted in holes on the outside of the wall and these can often still be seen today.

Defence from the front and above was not sufficient however, as the attackers could protect themselves in each instance, and it also required an uneconomic quantity of defenders. So stone towers were built, projecting from the circuit of the walls, which provided positions from which vigorous fire power could be directed on the flanks of besiegers as well. The stone towers might also be designed as small strongholds capable of resisting independently if the Bailey wall was taken. Stone throwing engines were also used by the defenders though only very strong towers could stand the vibrations as they worked. At best, their ammunition was specially prepared stone balls (typically 15" in diameter and 150 lbs. weight) which could be thrown several hundred yards. If these were not available, a wide variety of debris and even animal carcasses were thrown. At the siege of Kenilworth in 1264, such was the quantity of missiles employed by each side that they frequently collided in mid-air!

Trebuchet loaded with a dead horse.

If throwing engines were unobtainable or ineffective, the attackers had other methods at their disposal; one, the battering ram, was a heavy timber trunk with an iron head slung from the beams of a long

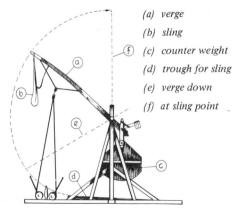

(a) *verge*

(b) *sling*

(c) *counter weight*

(d) *trough for sling*

(e) *verge down*

(f) *at sling point*

movable shed (penthouse) which gave protection to the men as they swung it against the castle wall.

Another method was to pick at the corners of towers until they weakened. In other instances the besiegers might drive a tunnel toward the walls, supporting the roof as they went with wooden props. Once they were underneath they lit a fire which burnt through the supports, causing the ground under the wall to collapse and cause a breach.

Direct assault on the castle using scaling ladders or huge movable towers (belfreys) was also common. The latter could only approach the wall after the castle ditch had been filled in (if there was one) and if the ground levels were suitable. Once there, a drawbridge at its top was lowered onto the castle parapet and soldiers poured out onto the walls.

Castles of the late twelfth and thirteenth centuries were able to resist new siege techniques to a remarkable degree by putting a series of walls between the keep and the field. The Bailey might be divided into an Inner and Outer Ward by a cross-wall complete with its own towers, ditch and gatehouse. Sometimes an Inner Bailey was wrapped round the Keep itself. Corners of walls and towers were rounded and thick spans added to their bases to combat picking, boring and battering. As mentioned above, Tower Keeps generally had a solid protective plinth at the base but, as a type, they were vulnerable at the corners. For instance, a corner of Rochester Keep was brought down by King John in the siege of 1216 and this was later rebuilt as a solid round turret. Because of this susceptibility at the corners, some Keeps came to be built with many strongly buttressed sides or even as completely round towers. This pattern was common on the continent where it is still known as a Donjon (the origin of our more sinister word, dungeon) and one of the most impressive examples in Britain is Bothwell in Lanarkshire. Another is at Pembroke, nearly complete and with its domed stone roof still in place.

Mangonel

The concept of the new castles was not entirely defensive. Most of them have more than one gateway even if the second is fairly small (known as the postern) from which surprise sorties could be made against the enemy. Some posterns are tiny and carefully concealed. These were useful in times of close siege to dispatch messengers and conduct other vital business under cover of night.

In front of many castle gates there can be seen a feature known as a Barbican. Its theory was to oblige an enemy to approach in such a way as to suit the defenders. Barbicans varied from simple earth foreworks to elaborate stone constructions with their own gatehouses and associated features. Thus, apart from a strongly fortified outer gate, intruders would find themselves approaching the castle in confined spaces and at angles most difficult for fighting. All this while they were attacked by the castle garrison from positions contrived especially to give them the advantage.

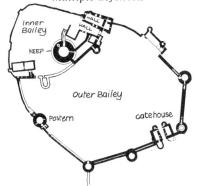

Pembroke Castle plan showing multiple defences.

We have now seen how stone castles evolved according to the demands of strategy and defence. But mention must also be made of the domestic buildings within the walls. The long Saxon Hall as seen in the Bayeux Tapestry might well have survived as a domestic addition to the first Motte and Bailey castles. Everyone ate and slept together in one place. Cooking was possible on a central fire whose smoke rose through a hole in the roof but in stone castles, a kitchen and storeroom are nearly always in close proximity to the hall. Fairly grand Halls with interior arcades of pillars and aisles exist at Oakham and Leicester whilst that of Winchester is larger and well suited to one of the ancient capitals of the kingdom. All these Halls are separate buildings however, and it was more usual for a Hall to lie up against the inside of the Bailey wall along with other offices of the castle.

The great Tower Keeps could not have been comfortable to live in as the emphasis was on defence and so one can observe a growing practice of building separate residential accommodation as an addition to their facilities. Where the castle had more than one Ward (or Bailey), therefore, a compact and comparatively safe group of buildings was planned and built against the inner wall. Some of the most fascinating parts of British castles are those domestic ranges which have a variety of features and stylish architectural detail too extensive to be discussed here. Two items need mention however, the Chapel and the castle Well.

All castles had a permanent place of worship even though this might only have been a small oratory within the thickness of a wall. Important castles, like Dover or Bramber, had a separate Church as a worshipping place for the garrison and some have spacious Chapels within the Keep or Gatehouse. It was a custom in those days for the younger son to enter the Church whilst his older brother inherited the Lordship. A link between church and castle then was almost inevitable. In fact some of the greatest Lords were prominent churchmen too. Some of the castle Chapels are indeed as memorable as the castles themselves; the 11th century Church of St.

Mary at Dover, the Chapel of St. John within London's White Tower or the mysterious and imposing Church of St. Mary de Castro at Leicester are fine examples.

In time of close siege a garrison often stood or fell by its store of provisions, for the fabric of a castle was often impregnable to all the works of its attackers who might then decide to try and starve it into surrendering. When Kenilworth was given up in 1265 for instance, it was because of the effects of disease and famine; it is even recorded that the victorious soldiers entering it were overcome by the awful stench inside! Because of the long time factor in mediaeval sieges a good and safe supply of water for the garrison was essential. Castle Wells were therefore often duplicated and strongly defended. Towers whose purpose was to contain the Well are common, as are very deep wells sunk within the walls of tower keeps. Piped water systems attached to wells, as at Dover, are rare however, and it is more usual to find several drawing points at different levels in the shaft. Amazingly, some water supplies in mediaeval castles still remain clear and uncontaminated and sometimes, as at Bodiam, an artesian well exists whose water rises to the surface on its own.

For all their strength, Tower Keeps had disadvantages which no amount of attached turrets or buttresses could eliminate. They were literally the place of last resort and rarely allowed the occupants a chance of escape as they were so often away from the perimeter walls of the castle. Being also uncomfortable to live in it is not surprising to see them dispensed with in the castles of the late thirteenth century. These were also built with different strategic objectives in mind which did not embrace the idea of a Keep in its existing form.

The new ideas are exemplified by those castles built for Edward 1 (1272 - 1307). His Welsh castles have rightly been described as some of the most magnificent and successful of the mediaeval world. They embody concepts which were important in military architecture for the next two hundred years and they perfectly suit particular local situations. None of them have Keeps; these are often replaced with equally powerful but more advanced Gatehouses, small Citadels capable of standing alone against attack. The castle gate therefore once more received the attention it had in the eleventh century as the part first to be strongly fortified.

Defences in the Gatehouse were many and various; Portcullises often came in threes or fours instead of ones or twos. These were interspaced with many pairs of doors and the vaults were pierced with 'murder holes' through which defenders were able to assail their attackers from above or pour water to extinguish fires lit to smoke them out (a favourite technique of mediaeval besiegers). To pass through some of these Gatehouses is really to enter a series of chambers each of which must be taken in turn. Additionally, the route might also take a right angle turn obliging attacking forces to regroup before proceeding. Often arrow slits in each side of the passage added to their discomfort. Sometimes a strong Keep-Gatehouse was added to an existing structure when it did in fact provide safe accommodation for the owner. Otherwise, one tower of the Curtain Walls might be made a self-sufficient strong point, like the Eagle Tower at Caernarvon or Martens Tower at Chepstow.

Edward I was the first English King to use mercenaries extensively. Whenever these soldiers appear in European history there are reports also of mutinies and defections and so the Edwardian Gatehouse can also be seen as a Keep for the personal safety of the Constable and a small band of regular men at arms. Some of Edward's castles also demonstrate a development in the idea of defence in depth, mentioned concerning the stone castles of the early thirteenth century. Now there is a symmetrical arrangement of one Bailey within the other, the inner one completely overlooking and commanding the outer so that their assailants were met with fire from multiple fighting platforms and would also be at a disadvantage if they occupied the outer walls. If they penetrated the Gatehouse, the space within the two walls could be-

Concentric castle

come for them a death trap as they proceeded to the even tougher defences before them.

These concentric castles as they are called, of which the largest is the Tower of London, the most perfect Beaumaris, and the grandest and most beautiful Caerphilly, were expensive, and except for the latter they were only built by the King. A most effective and feasible alternative for other landowners however was an extension of this Keep/Gatehouse idea into a rectangular castle having only one line of defence. The Curtain Wall was laid out in the symmetrical fashion of a concentric castle with strong towers at the corners and at the mid-point of the walls. These compact and comparatively small fortresses, though appearing uncompromisingly tough and military from the outside, show an interesting plan inside. Here the lord's quarters were not contained in the Gatehouse but spread round the walls. A duplicate unit was provided for the men at arms, a distinction partly brought about by the unreliable qualities of the mercenaries noted above.

A rectangular or square plan remained

the pattern for new castles until the end of the fifteenth century and the Gatehouse, whilst remaining a strong point, formed part of a balanced architectural whole. Sometimes though, they remain as the outstanding strong feature of what is really a fortified house (Donnington or Oxburgh Hall) and herald the last phase of castle building in England.

The latest English castles have about them a most satisfying calm combined with strength which must spring from a wish to design for appearance sake as well as for domestic comfort and defence. The brick castles of Kirby Muxloe and Herstmonceux present a time-tested form of defence, with a strong Gatehouse in the centre of one wall which is supported at each end by strong corner towers. The rectangle is completed in the usual manner with corner and middle towers in the other three sides. Provision was made for ordnance but practical defence was to be offered by crossbow or longbow across a wide moat. The whole concept obliged an attacker to approach at a disadvantage, the emphasis being that, in the true mediaeval manner, he had to enter the castle to take it.

17

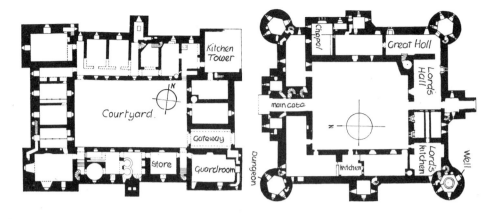

Rectangular plan castles showing domestic buildings.

A few remarkable buildings stand out from the general trend; two of these are Ashby de la Zouche in England and Raglan in Wales. At Ashby, in 1474, the Great Yorkist, Lord Hastings, added a strong residential Tower House 90 ft. high, to a lightly fortified castle. The comparatively passive and well appointed building was nevertheless so well able to resist attack that even in 1644 Parliamentary forces were unable to take it. In concept, it has much in common with Scottish Tower Houses although the remains of the fortified Manor House which it dominates are larger and more elaborate than might be found in Scotland.

Raglan is a most beautiful castle, whose domestic apartments were a wonder of their time (the middle and late fifteenth century) and it too has a Great Tower commanding all. Yet this Great Tower, standing alone and surrounded by a Moat, is a strangely retrograde feature, for the strategy of such isolated structures lies with the ideas of two hundred years before. Nevertheless, Raglan too resisted a heavy siege in the Civil War in an age when all mediaeval castles might well have been considered outmoded.

The fact is that castles could only serve a purpose in troubled times and those were when powerful men built them. The Civil War was a gap in otherwise well ordered times; Englishmen began to look outside their own country for new wealth and power and the energy devoted in the past to building fortified houses was diverted to building homes demonstrating their worldly taste and containing the furniture and paintings, sculpture, porcelain and carpets which they acquired abroad. If their existing house was a castle they often altered it to suit their new requirements. Many English castles received this treatment and are still lived in today. For every one of these however, there are dozens of imposing uninhabited remains which are monuments to the social and military life of the Middle Ages. A visit to any one of them is likely to be both recreational and instructive, well worth both the small effort and cost it entails.

Tim Andrews

THE DEVELOPMENT OF ORDNANCE
AND THE CASTLES OF HENRY VIII

It has often been assumed that the invention of cannon brought about the end of castle building. Whilst this is partly true, other important factors were the growth of strong government under the Tudor monarchs which in turn brought security and peace to the community. In fact, Henry VIII (1509 - 1547) issued the last licence to crenellate, for Cowdray in Sussex, but the results are so far from what we call a castle as to make the document an expression of its owner's pride rather than his intention.

Guns are known to have existed in warfare from 1327. Many castles were fitted to take them and indeed they were used as early as 1342 at the siege of Stirling. Their firing rate was slow, however, as they needed cleaning between each discharge and they were disappointingly inaccurate. It is recorded, for instance, that two cannons in action at the siege of Ypres in 1383 fired 450 rounds in one day without injuring a single man! For a long time they were also inclined to be a dangerous liability to their users because of the frequency with which they burst. For this reason only a small charge could be used which shot a flighted bolt. Even when manufacturers were able to make siege guns capable of discharging heavy stones with great force this danger remained. King James II of Scotalnd, who had a great interest in developing the new devices, was killed when one blew up as he observed it in operation at the siege of Roxburgh in 1460.

The design of mediaeval walls and towers, developed with the arching trajectory of Mangonels and Trebuchets in mind, could not withstand the horizontal battering produced by siege guns which appeared in the middle of the 15th century. In 1424, the city of Le Mans was besieged by the English who brought up their "great goones". These were hardly known in France at the time and their efforts "so shaked, crushed and rived the walles that within few days the citie was despoyled of all her tours and outward defences". The great weapons often acquired proper names and almost national fame. One, "Mons Meg", made in 1455 was painted red, lovingly attended and continuously in service in Scotland over a great number of years. It is recorded that in 1539 she apparently fired a "bullet" just over two miles and it was not until 1680, when she burst whilst firing a salute, that she was finally taken out of action to be repaired and kept at Edinburgh castle, where she still stands.

Despite the success of "Mons" and her relations, the principal hand armaments remained the crossbow and longbow and, despite the presence of ordnance at the Battle of Flodden in 1513, it was still the longbow which won the day for Henry VIII. Of course masonry could be adapted against the new weapons and, certainly, existing castles were not at first made obsolete by these developments. In the Civil War many mediaeval fortresses held out against persistant and lengthy cannonades and it was this characteristic which chiefly persuaded the Parliamentary government to dismantle and blow them up, hence the ruins in profusion still gracing our countryside.

Actually, the first artillery was Henry's monopoly, its chief exponents usually being imported from Flanders or Germany, and he constructed the first castles specifically designed for it.

The Coastal Forts of Henry VIII differ from other Royal castles in that they were

St. Mawes

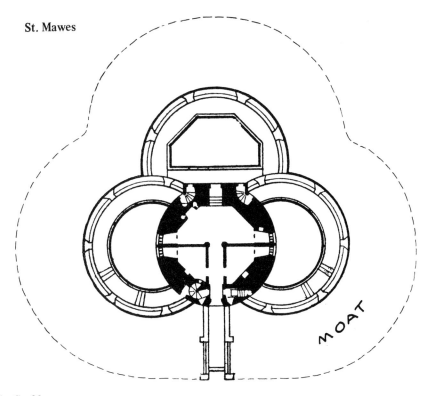

left: St. Mawes
above: Ground plan

the first to be built by the Monarch for the sole purpose of protecting the state. They were not conceived in a period of civil unrest but as a defence against the possible invasion of the Emperor Charles V and Francois I, King of France. They are not mere gun emplacements, however, and they retain many characteristics of the mediaeval castle whose design had to anticipate open assault. Extensive outworks were built, often including a moat, and gateways were defended by a drawbridge, portcullis and so on. Inside, whilst the design centred round the need to direct and serve large guns, familiar devices were employed to check intruders — the route into the Keep at Deal, for instance, is particularly ingenious.

Seen as a group, the most interesting feature of these castles is the variation of symmetrical patterns, consisting of circles, triangles, diamonds and other geometrical shapes, which their plans display. In elevation, the designers achieved a low profile with rounded and sloping parapets to the walls. These reverted to the great thicknesses found in castles of the thirteenth century and offered various planes to deflect the cannon balls fired at them. Though defence was possible at the parapet, the main apertures in the walls are huge embrasures, splayed out to present a good field of fire for the guns mounted inside. In addition, smaller gun loops were also provided, generally giving complete command of the area immediately outside the walls.

21

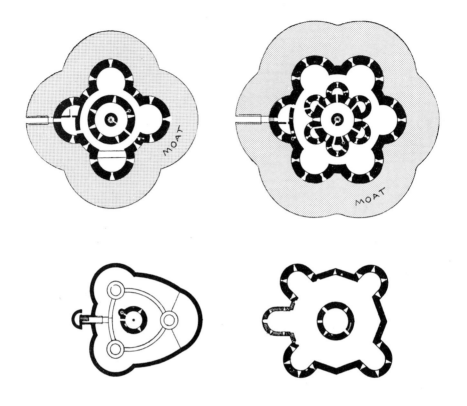

Building accounts for some of the castles survive – Sandgate cost a total of £5,543-19-3¾d ! – and we know that the architect for those in Kent was a German, one Stefan von Haschenperg. Many of them are in good condition and sited in interesting and accessible locations stretching from Cornwall to the Thames Estuary.

In concept, Henry's Coastal Forts presage the channel defence system developed against the threat of Napoleonic invasion two hundred and fifty years later, indeed they played their part then, but in many details they still bear a close resemblance to the castles which they superceded.

Tim Andrews

Plans illustrating the geometric character of Henry VIII's castles.

ENGLAND

ORKNEY

SHETLAND

CAITH

SUTHERLAND

ROSS AND CROMARTY

MORAY

NAIRN

BANFF

ABERDEEN

INVERNESS

KINC

ANGUS

PERTHS

ARGYLL

KINR

FIFE

DUNB

CLACK

STIR

RENF

W.LOTH

M.LOTH

E.LOTH

BER

LANARKS

PEEBL

SELK

BUTE

AYRS

ROX

NORTHLD

DUMF

WIG

KIRKCUD

CUMB

DURHAM

WESTMLD

ISLE OF MAN

YORKSHIRE

LANCASHIRE

LINCS

ANGL

FLINTS

CHESHIRE

DERBYS

CAERN

DENB

NOTTS

MER

NORFOLK

MONT

STAFFS

LEICS

RUT

HUNTS

SHROPS

RAD

WARKS

NORTHANTS

SUFFOLK

CARD

WORCS

CANBS

PEMB

HEREFS

BEDS

CARM

BRECON

OXON

HERTS

ESSEX

GLAM

MON

GLOS

BUCKS

LONDON

BERKS

SURREY

KENT

WILTS

SOMERSET

HANTS

SUSSEX

DEVON

DORSET

CORNWALL

BERKSHIRE

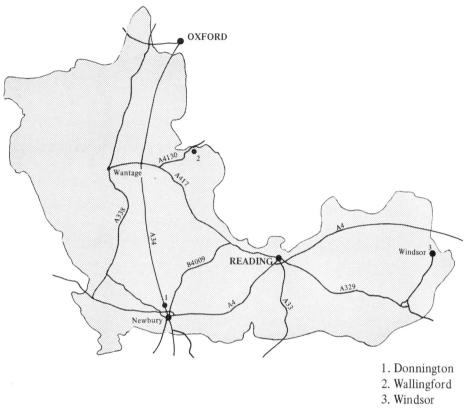

1. Donnington
2. Wallingford
3. Windsor

Licensed in 1386, Donnington Castle saw its greatest days during the Civil War when it withstood a twenty months' siege before finally surrendering to the Parliamentary forces.

The lines can still be traced of the fantastic earthworks which were built for the castle's defence in 1643—4 by Colonel Boys at a cost of £1,000, their 'star' shape with projecting gun emplacements giving maximum coverage to defenders without unduly exposing them to attack.

WALLINGFORD

Privately owned and the property of Sir John Hedges, C.B.E., Wallingford Castle was used as a Royal residence from the thirteenth to the sixteenth century, after which time it began to fall into decay.

Little now remains of the building for, although it was refortified during the Civil War, it was captured by the Parliamentarians in 1646 and, in 1652, it was ordered to be demolished. Clearly, however, it was of the Motte and Bailey type, well defended on one side by earthworks and on the other by the Thames, and it was twice besieged by Stephen during his wars with the Empress Matilda during the twelfth century, a Charter of Privileges being granted to the town in 1155 by Henry II in recognition of the loyalty shown to himself and his mother.

England's largest complete castle, Windsor is quite worthy to have been the sole subject of the number of books written about it.

Begun about 1070, Windsor Castle was intended as a means of controlling the middle reaches of the Thames and as one of a number of fortifications placed within a day's march of London, taking its name from the earlier Saxon residence at Windlesora, an ancient settlement some three miles distant. Doubtless, the original castle was simply a wooden construction which was later enlarged and, about a century later, improved and made more permanent by the use of stone from Bedfordshire quarries.

Successive sovereigns altered and enlarged the castle which has remained a Royal residence to this day, although the private apartments were, until the nineteenth century, housed along the Northern side of the Upper Ward, where they were originally sited for reasons of defence. It was King George IV who rebuilt the Southern and Eastern flanks of this Ward in order to accommodate the private apartments which are currently used by the British Sovereign.

Although the Castle Precincts are open to the public all the year round, from 10 a.m. until sunset, the State Apartments are open only when the Queen is not in residence and, since the dates vary from year to year, intending visitors would be advised to enquire beforehand.

CHESHIRE

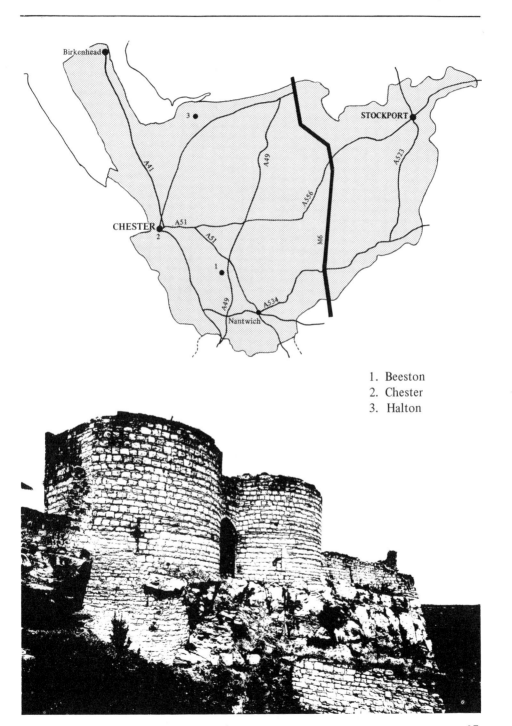

1. Beeston
2. Chester
3. Halton

BEESTON CASTLE

Seven hundred and forty feet above sea level rises the isolated rock upon which stands the castle built by Randle Blundeville, Earl of Chester, in 1220. Although Beeston Castle is extensively ruined, the inner gatehouse is still fairly well preserved and the remains can still be seen of the Outer Bailey curtain and seven semicircular towers, though the domestic buildings, which were situated against the curtains, have gone.

Beeston Castle is particularly interesting by reason of the fact that it contained no Keep, its builders relying on the natural inaccessibility of the site for their main defence. They did, however, cut a very fine rock ditch which can still be seen between the Baileys.

CHESTER

Founded by the Conqueror on an earlier Saxon site, Chester Castle was given stone walls and towers by Henry III in the thirteenth century, though much of the mediaeval masonry was removed by Thomas Harrison between 1789 and 1813 to make way for the Grand Entrance and the Assize Courts which he built in its place. The square Agricola Tower, however, dates from the thirteenth century and contains a rather nice chapel dedicated to St. Mary de Castro.

The walls, slighted by the Parliamentarians, have been largely rebuilt to incorporate much of the Roman work to be seen on the site and, although built mainly as a perambulatory platform, contain a number of towers of which the Water Tower is interesting.

Admission to the castle is free, though opening times are at the discretion of the Military authorities.

HALTON

Although there are only fragmentary remains of Halton Castle, the views commanded by the rocky hill upon which it stands ensure a steady flow of visitors to the site.

Built by Nigel, Baron of Halton, the castle was the residence of subsequent Barons, who were also Constables of Chester and was used as the place of trial and punishment for offenders from a wide surrounding area. During the Elizabethan period, Halton was used as a prison for recusants. Under Charles I it was fortified and garrisoned against the Parliamentary forces who, commanded by Sir William Brereton, captured and slighted it in 1646, since when it has been allowed to fall rather more peaceably into decay.

CORNWALL

1. Launceston
2. Pendennis
3. Pengersick
4. Restormel
5. St. Catherine's
6. St. Mawes
7. St. Michael's Mount
8. Tintagel
9. Trematon

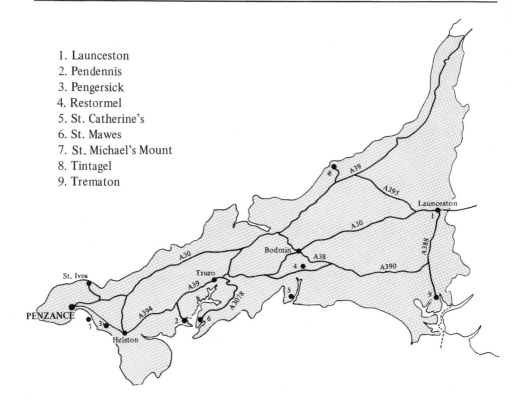

LAUNCESTON

Robert of Mortain was the brother of William the Conqueror and it was here, at Launceston, that he established his headquarters.

The castle, mentioned in Domesday, is unusual especially in that the circular Keep on a mound contains a higher, round tower which was a later addition.

Although the castle's teeth have been drawn somewhat by the municipal landscaping which surrounds the ruin, it remains an interesting and very pleasant spot enhanced by the recent excavations carried out which have revealed the well and the drawbridge pit to the keep barbican.

Restormel castle.

PENDENNIS

Pendennis Castle, with that of St. Mawes, formed part of the chain of coastal defences built by Henry VIII at the time when he was convinced that Britain was going to be forcibly persuaded to join the European Community.

Many of these small fortresses remain and it is interesting to observe the number of variations of design there were constructed with the same basic elements.

Built toward the middle of the sixteenth century, Pendennis Castle was enlarged during the second half of the century by Henry's daughter, Queen Elizabeth I. The Civil War saw its moment of triumph when, after being blockaded for five months by land and sea, the garrison rode out with colours flying.

RESTORMEL

Restormel Castle was founded about 1100, though the circular, shell keep probably dates from the following century. Its large size (110ft. diameter) is remarkable and it contains all the necessary domestic apartments which were built in the usual, lean-to manner against its walls.

There is also an interesting pit with traces of a passage leading off it. Little information is available concerning the purpose of this feature and, although it might have been designed as a cool store for perishable foodstuffs, other, more sinister purposes can be ascribed to it.

A stroll round the wall walk is most rewarding for the fine views across the River Fowey and surrounding countryside.

Above: St. Mawes castle. Below: St. Catherine's castle, Fowey.

ST. CATHERINE'S, FOWEY

ST. MAWES

Built by Thomas Treffrey for Henry VIII circa 1540, St. Catherine's Castle is another in the line of sea defences built during this period and was named after the Chapel on the cliffs built by a fourteenth century Prior of Tywardreath.

During the wars with the Dutch, the Castle defended, in 1666, the Virginia Fleet sheltering in Fowey Harbour, suffering very little damage and only one fatality during the engagement. Many of the cannonballs fired during that battle were collected from the surrounding countryside during the years that followed and most of these were deposited in Fowey Church.

Manned during the Napoleonic wars and again during the Second World War, the castle is now in the hands of the Department of the Environment.

Built by Thomas Treffry, Governor of St. Mawes, this fortress resembles that of St. Catherine's which Treffry also built at about the same time, though it is not sited so magnificently.

For those who like their castles detached, in a beautiful state of decorative repair and equipped with all main services, St. Michael's Mount, in Mount's Bay, would seem to be the perfect spot; it even contains a model of itself made entirely from champagne corks by a gentleman who buttled there in the days when no self-respecting butler would make models from any other material.

The excellent and lavishly illustrated guide book to the castle contains a wealth of legendary and historical information about the building itself and the rock upon which it stands, tracing the history of the building from the time St. Michael the Archangel is said to have appeared in a vision to a group of fishermen on the island in 495, thus making the rock a place of pilgrimage, to the present day.

Although not as perfect as Restormel, Trematon Castle is, nevertheless, one of the most impressive of the Cornish castles and much of the credit for this must go to the superb site which commands truly magnificent views.

The shell keep tends to be nearer oval than round (doubtless following the contours of the ground on which it was built) and the parapet is complete.

St. Michael's Mount.

TINTAGEL

The wild and romantic countryside around Tintagel contains all the elements from which legends are made — hardly surprising, therefore, to find that Tintagel Castle is said to have been built over the birthplace of King Arthur.

Now only a minimal ruin, this historic building has been split in two by the encroaching sea. Part of the castle stands on the mainland — the Main Gateway and Outer Courtyard are still to be seen — while the Inner Court and the remains of the Hall are perched on a small island whose separation from the mainland is documented from the thirteenth century when a bridge was required to pass from one part of the castle to the other.

By the sixteenth century the castle no longer tenable on account of the widening gap, was abandoned and left to gather further legends as decay and the passage of time caused people to forget its true origins.

CUMBERLAND

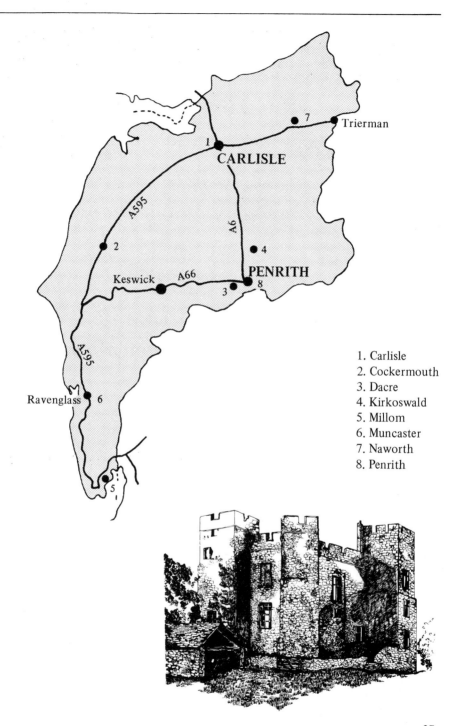

1. Carlisle
2. Cockermouth
3. Dacre
4. Kirkoswald
5. Millom
6. Muncaster
7. Naworth
8. Penrith

Built to guard the western end of the Scottish border, Carlisle Castle was a place of great strategic importance in its early days.

Originally a timber built structure, the first Norman Castle was thrown up in 1092 by William Rufus, being superseded by stone walls and keep from 1157. Of this building, the keep still remains but there have been many repairs and additions to the rest of the castle dating from various periods right up to the time of Henry VIII, who built the Citadel and adapted parts of the castle for artillery.

The Keep is now used to house a museum of the former Border Regiment.

Cockermouth Castle is believed to date from the twelfth century, though we are told that the original stone castle was almost totally destroyed in 1221 as a result of the political treachery of William de Fortibus who was a signatory of Magna Carta.

Rebuilding commenced some four years later and subsequent owners added buildings and walls over the years — mainly between the thirteenth and fifteenth centuries, though the castle was reported as being '. . . in grayte decaie' by 1578.

That this decay was not too far advanced can be gathered from the information we have concerning the castle's defence by Royalist forces during the Civil War, their surrender proving the signal for the castle's destruction by the Parliamentary forces.

Carlisle castle

Cockermouth castle.

DACRE CASTLE

An early fourteenth century pele tower, Dacre Castle was built in the shape of a cube with a projection at each corner. Two of these are in the form of square towers and the others are more buttress-like.

A licence for a chapel in the castle was granted in 1354.

Dacre castle.

KIRK OSWALD

Just a single great tower, containing a spiral staircase, and a couple of chunks of heavy masonry are all that remain of Kirk Oswald Castle which was continuously occupied for five hundred years before finally being abandoned to the wind, weather and the attentions of local builders in need of stone.

A fine fourteenth century carved ceiling from Kirk Oswald is to be seen at Naworth Castle.

MILLOM

The Lords of Millom were granted their licence to crenellate in 1334 and their castle stands, ruined, on an eminence about a mile from the centre of the town.

A square tower added by a Tudor owner is now used as a farmhouse, the rest of the castle having fallen into the state of picturesque decay so beloved by eighteenth and nineteenth century romantics.

MUNCASTER

Close to the village of Ravenglass, Muncaster Castle is situated in some of the most magnificent of northern English country.

Said to have been built on the site of an earlier Roman Fort, the castle dates from the early fourteenth century, though it was extensively rebuilt during the nineteenth century and the stately rooms contain fine collections of furniture and objets d'art for the pleasure of visitors.

The tower in the grounds of Muncaster castle.

Muncaster castle

Naworth castle.

NAWORTH

This fine castle was built following the granting of Ranulph of Dacre's licence to crenellate in 1335.

Standing on a spur of land which falls away from the castle walls on three sides, the site was doubtless chosen for its defensive qualities, though it commands some extremely attractive views across the surrounding country.

Following a great fire in 1844, the interior of the castle was extensively rebuilt by Salvin, though reference to old prints shows that he made virtually no alterations to its exterior appearance.

PENRITH

The ruins of Penrith Castle are still quite impressive despite their advanced state of decay.

Dating from the fourteenth century, Penrith Castle was built for William Strickland, later Bishop of Carlisle and Archbishop of Canterbury. Unfortunately, as a result of its ruinous state, virtually nothing is known of the interior arrangements of the structure and the remaining sections of wall stand in a park, open at the discretion of the Urban District Council.

DERBYSHIRE

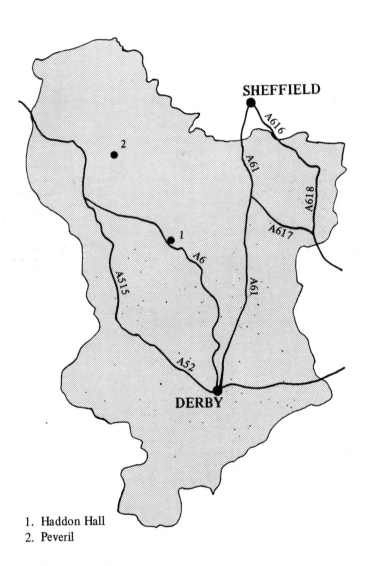

1. Haddon Hall
2. Peveril

HADDON HALL, BAKEWELL

This justly praised, romantic, lovable, rambling old castle is the Derbyshire seat of the Duke of Rutland and is open to the public during the summer from Tuesday to Saturday and, on Bank Holiday weekends from Easter to the late summer Bank Holiday, on Sundays and Mondays as well.

It is kept in the most beautiful condition and houses some magnificent tapestries and period furniture beside being well equipped with the usual range of oddities and curios with which all ancestral homes seem to abound. Parts of the building date from the eleventh century, when William Peveril, an illegitimate son of William the Conqueror, held this and several other manors in Derbyshire, but much of the existing structure has been built by succeeding generations.

For about two hundred years, from the second half of the seventeenth century, Haddon Hall stood empty and had it not been for the fact that the 9th Duke (the present Duke's father) devoted his life to the restoration of the building to as near as possible the state which it must have been in its prime, this might well have been another of those ruins which, although interesting, tend to leave the visitor with a feeling of wondering sadness. So well have the restorations been effected, however, that Haddon Hall cannot fail to delight every visitor whether he be historical scholar or curious sightseer.

PEVERIL

Peveril Castle stands atop a steep, rounded hill above the tourist village of Castleton, where it vies with portholes and caves as an attraction to visitors.

Built by William Peveril, Bailiff and illegitimate son of the Conqueror, this is the only truly important castle to have been built in Derbyshire and its interest lies, in part, in the fact that it appears to have been built originally of stone instead of supplanting a timber palisade. Evidence of this is to be found in the remaining north Curtain Wall, where the stonework can be seen to be of the early herringbone pattern.

The Keep, erected on the highest point of the site dates from 1176 when it was commissioned by Henry II and it has been suggested that the gateway in the northeast angle also dates from this period.

It is interesting to note that a considerable amount of Roman brick was used in the construction of both these features.

By the end of the fourteenth century, Peveril Castle had lost its importance and, within the following three centuries, it fell into ruins. Despite its ruined state, however, the castle retains a certain air of lofty strength, an impression which is heightened by its siting in the rugged countryside overlooking Carr Dale and Peak Cavern.

DEVON

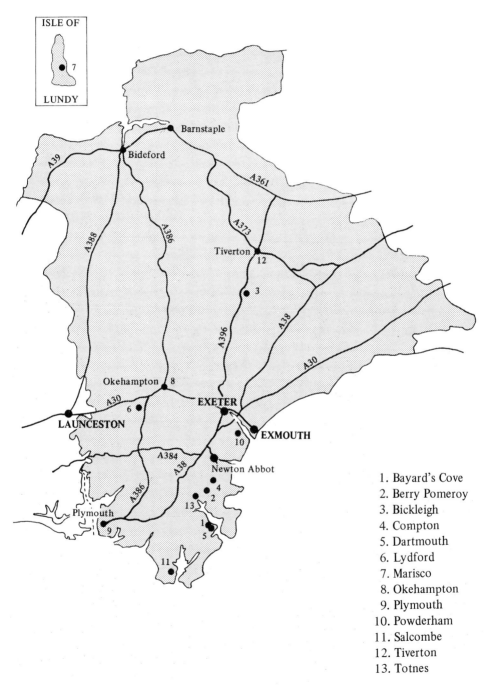

ISLE OF

7

LUNDY

Barnstaple

Bideford

A39

A361

A373

A388

A386

Tiverton

12

3

A396

A38

A30

Okehampton 8

A30

6

EXETER

LAUNCESTON

10 EXMOUTH

A384

A38

Newton Abbot

A386

4

13 2

Plymouth

1

9 5

11

1. Bayard's Cove
2. Berry Pomeroy
3. Bickleigh
4. Compton
5. Dartmouth
6. Lydford
7. Marisco
8. Okehampton
9. Plymouth
10. Powderham
11. Salcombe
12. Tiverton
13. Totnes

BAYARDS COVE

This small sea fort was built as an artillery work pure and simple but, for some reason, the gun ports were designed with such a limited field of fire that the structure was obsolete before its completion.

BERRY POMEROY

The older part of Berry Pomeroy dates back to the 1300s and comprises the Gatehouse St. Margaret's Tower and parts of the Curtain Wall built by the de Pomerois family.

This was later extended by the Seymours, Sir Edward and Edward, who in the sixteenth and seventeenth centuries added the living quarters round a courtyard to the east and the Offices, Kitchens and other rooms to the north, all in the beautifully elegant style of the Tudor period.

BICKLEIGH

Another stronghold of the Courtenay family, Bickleigh Castle dates mainly from the fifteenth century.

There is a Norman Chapel by the river outside the Gatehouse and the Gatehouse, with its vaulted gateway of pink sandstone is interestingly massive. Apart from these features, the fragments of the remains are mostly Tudor.

COMPTON

Compton Castle is one of those extensively restored and furnished buildings beloved of the National Trust.

Compton dates mainly from the fourteenth to the sixteenth century and, with a single break of one hundred and thirty years, it has remained in the hands of the Gilbert family.

Apart from the undeniably attractive appearance and character of the house as it is today, much of the interest of Compton lies in its connections with Sir Walter Raleigh and Sir Richard Grenville, both branches of the Gilbert family tree, and many other members of that illustrious family.

Compton castle.

46

Above: Dartmouth castle. Below: Lydford castle.

DARTMOUTH

Although there are some fourteenth century remains, the greater part of the ruin of Dartmouth Castle dates from the fifteenth and sixteenth centuries.

Established to provide a stout defence for the harbour at Dartmouth, the castle was well equipped with artillery and, in 1667, the defences were strong enough to deter the Dutch fleet from attacking the harbour.

An interesting feature is the opening through which a chain was passed to be fastened right across the harbour mouth.

LYDFORD

Although in Devon, Lydford and Dartmoor are part of the Duchy of Cornwall.

The original Castle at Lydford was, as is usual, a timber structure with earthworks and the existing building dates from the twelfth century. Small, square and neat, it is said to have been built as a prison. The castle was also used by the Stannary Court to administer justice for the local tin mines. 'Lydford Law' became euphemism for rough justice.

47

Marisco castle on Lundy Island.

MARISCO CASTLE, LUNDY ISLAND

Although called Marisco Castle, there is some doubt that the building was erected by the family of that name, some authorities suggesting that the fort was built by Henry III following the downfall of the de Mariscos. In either event, it is probable that the Castle was built early in the thirteenth century after which it fell into decay for, by the time of the Civil Wars, it had to be completely renovated in order to be garrisoned for the Royalist cause.

By the end of the eighteenth century, the castle was extensively damaged and, early in the nineteenth century, some Irish labourers brought to the Island by Sir Aubrey de Vere Hunt removed all the remaining woodwork to be used as fuel for their fires.

All that now remains of the original buildings are the decayed shells of some cottages and traces of courtyard and steps.

OKEHAMPTON

This superb ruin in beautiful surroundings has, if the old records are to be believed, remained virtually unchanged in appearance for over two hundred years.

Built on the site of an earlier (and probably wooden) construction established by Baldwin Fitzgilbert during the reign of William the Conqueror, the castle dates from the late thirteenth and early fourteenth centuries when the Courtenay family fully secured the Earldom of Devon. Over the following two centuries, the Courtenays successively lost and regained their holdings as a result of various political dealings until, in 1538, Earl Henry was beheaded and the castle ordered to be dismantled.

Since 1967, the castle has been in the capable hands of the Department of the Environment whose skilled care will ensure that it remains in as good condition as it is possible to keep it.

48

In R. N. Worth's History of Plymouth (1890) we read that 'The castle was built on the rocky spur at the eastern end of the Hoe, immediately overlooking and commanding the entrance of Sutton Pool, somewhere in the reign of Henry IV.'

The few remains of the castle are now to be found incorporated in the Citadel which was built during the reign of Charles II and, although the surviving building is of interest as an example of a military building, it does not fall within the definition of Castles which were, by the seventeenth century, militarily outmoded.

Described in the National Trust guide book as 'The Historic Home of the Courtenay Family', Powderham Castle dates in part from the late fourteenth/early fifteenth centuries, though alterations carried out during the eighteenth and nineteenth centuries serve very well to disguise that fact.

More of a stately home than a castle, Powderham is the home of the Earl of Devon who is a direct descendant of the original builder, Sir Philip Courtenay.

Okehampton castle.

TIVERTON, DEVON

The ample remains of this castle, another of the Courtenay strongholds, date, in part, from the thirteenth century and suggest that the castle was built in a quadrangular shape, with angle towers.

Although it is very much a ruin, enough remains to convince the visitor that this must once have been an imposing and extremely strong building, although the pink sandstone of which it was built has eroded nicely into rather soft-looking shapes.

As was so often the case, the castle's destruction followed the defeat of its garrison by Parliamentary forces during the Civil War.

The gracious house which is now called Tiverton Castle dates from the early years of the eighteenth century when the ruin was bought by a wealthy wool merchant, Peter West, who used the stone from the castle to build his house within the remains of the main court. This house is now open to the public by previous written appointment only.

TOTNES, DEVON

Built by Judhael, leader of the Conqueror's Southwestern campaign, Totnes Castle is the proud possessor of one of the largest mottes in Britain.

A remarkably complete example of Norman military building, the castle was built during the early part of the thirteenth century and its shell keep rebuilt during the fourteenth century.

Totnes Castle

DORSET

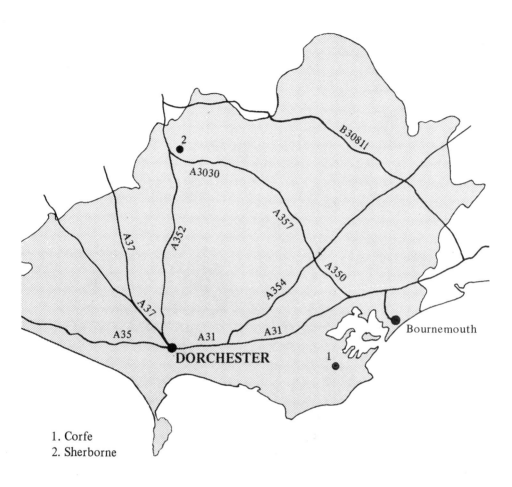

1. Corfe
2. Sherborne

Corfe Castle has a history which traces back to the days before the Norman Conquest, though it was probably a royal hunting lodge in the Saxon days.

Rising high above the town of Corfe, this must be one of the most picturesque, romantic, imposing ruins in the entire country. Ivy grown and pierced with elegant windows, it is difficult to imagine that these walls echoed to the cries of 24 knights whom King John imprisoned and starved until 22 of them died. Also held captive here were Prince Arthur's sister, Eleanor and the daughters of a one time King of Scotland, Isabel and Margery.

Edward II was also imprisoned here for a time before his murder in Berkeley Castle.

During the Civil Wars, the castle was in the hands of the Bankes family who declared for the King and it was twice besieged, being eventually betrayed by a member of its own garrison who opened a gate at night to allow the attacking forces entry. The castle was then slighted by order of Parliament, though its walls were so strongly fashioned that they sustained far less damage than those of other, less sturdy castles undergoing similar treatment.

SHERBORNE

The Old Castle at Sherborne lies just across the lake, to the north of what is now known as Sherborne Castle which was begun by Sir Walter Raleigh after, the story goes, he had tried to convert the old Keep into a modern dwelling as befitted a man of his rank.

Although, doubtless, a considerable amount of stone was removed from the old castle to form part of the fabric of the later house, much of the building and surrounding country must be in a state little altered from the days when Raleigh made his home there.

Above: The new castle at Sherborne. Below: 'Old' Sherborne castle.

DURHAM

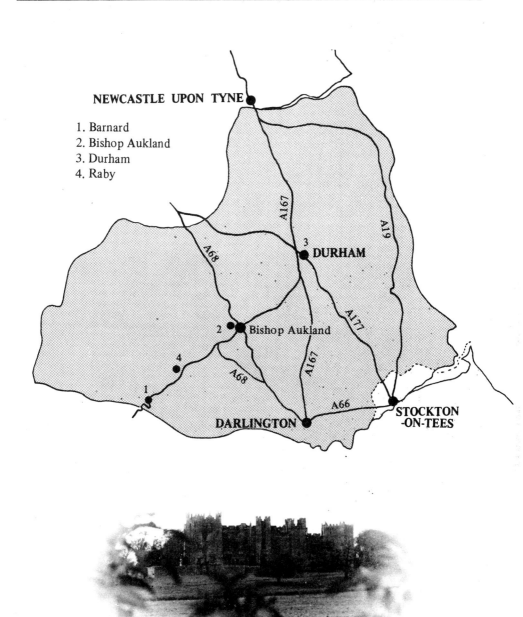

NEWCASTLE UPON TYNE

1. Barnard
2. Bishop Aukland
3. Durham
4. Raby

A167

A19

A68

3 DURHAM

A177

2 Bishop Aukland

A68

4

1

A167

A66

DARLINGTON

STOCKTON
-ON-TEES

Upon a rocky promontory overlooking the River Tees, Barnard Castle looks ivy grown, ruined and rather shabby when viewed from the road on the Western side.

Under the custodianship of the Department of the Environment, however, the Castle is revealed to be excellently maintained. Large and smoothly lawned, it has been encroached upon through the centuries by householders who have claimed parts of its precincts for their gardens. The Curtain wall, too, has been incorporated into a number of dwellings built, most probably, of stone scavenged from the castle ruins during the late seventeenth and early eighteenth centuries.

Built by Bernard Baliol in the late eleventh or early twelfth century, this was once an extremely important stronghold jealously sought by the Bishops of Durham who wished to include it in the possessions of their See.

The Baliol family ensured the endurance of their name through the foundation of Baliol College, Oxford, by John Baliol and his wife Devorguilla, through whose right John was also Regent of Scotland. Upon his death, his two eldest sons having predeceased him, his younger son, also John, inherited the Castle and estates and was, in 1292, crowned King of Scotland at Scone. After forming an alliance with the King of France, he fell from favour in England and his estates were forfeit to the Crown. At this point, the Bishop of Durham, Bishop Bek, stepped in and seized the castle and held it from 1296 to 1301 before he was relieved of his palatinate.

Militarily, the Castle saw its most important days during the rising of the Northern Earls when it withstood a siege of eleven days before being treacherously betrayed by some of the townspeople.

By the sixteenth century, the castle was showing signs of disrepair and in 1630, it was largely dismantled, all articles of value being carried off to Raby Castle.

BISHOP AUCKLAND

A consequence of Bishop Bek's ambition, the Castle at Bishop Auckland began life as a Norman Manor House but was converted by his Lordship into the nucleus of the castle which now stands on the site.

Successive Bishops enlarged and improved the castle and, during the Commonwealth, it was confiscated by Parliament who sold it to Sir Arthur Haselrigg who demolished parts of it and built himself a mansion within the old courtyard.

Bishop Cosin, upon the castle's return to the See of Durham after the Restoration, set to and restored or rebuilt much of the castle and this work was continued by later Bishops, many of whom made additions of their own.

Charles I visited the castle a number of times, the last as a prisoner two years before his execution in 1649.

Many famous Bishops are buried in the Chapel which was converted from the original Norman Hall by Bishop Cosin and which, after falling into disrepair, was redecorated and dedicated in 1888.

DURHAM

In 1069, William the Conqueror determined to build a stout castle at Durham to act as a centre for the palatinate which he was establishing as a buffer against the wild Scots.

The scheme worked well, particularly since the palatinate was under the command of a Bishop appointed by the King, and the resultant group of buildings, Castle and Cathedral, high above the River Wear, form an impressive centrepiece to the fusion of ecclesiastical and temporal power which they symbolise.

From 1072 until the foundation, in 1831, of Durham university, the Castle was the fortress residence of the Bishops of Durham and, as might be expected, their various Lordships added a piece here and altered a piece there so that, over the years, the castle has entirely changed in size and appearance since its first building in stone during the reign of William Rufus (1087–1100).

Predictably, the building contains some very fine examples of architecture from various periods, particularly the Norman Gallery built by Bishop Pudsey in the twelfth century, the Norman Chapel (11th century), Bishop Cosin's Staircase (1663) and the Great Hall built by Bishop Beck in about 1300 which has since been enlarged and reduced again to its original size.

RABY CASTLE

Raby Castle, seat of the Lord Barnard, is another of the country's magnificent, rambling, beautifully kept Stately Homes.

Dating in part from the fourteenth century, Raby Castle has seen many events of great importance in the shaping of the nation's history, including the plotting of the famous Rising of the North in the cause of Mary Queen of Scots. Major additions and alterations were made to the fabric of the castle in the eighteenth and nineteenth centuries, notably the octagonal Tower (which was built by William Burn who

pulled down the South end of the Baron's Hall and carried out other work in the years following 1842).

The interior of the castle is crammed with fabulous furniture and pictures, the ten acres of gardens are beautifully tended and the stables house a tea room and an exhibition of horse drawn vehicles from the eighteenth and nineteenth centuries.

ESSEX

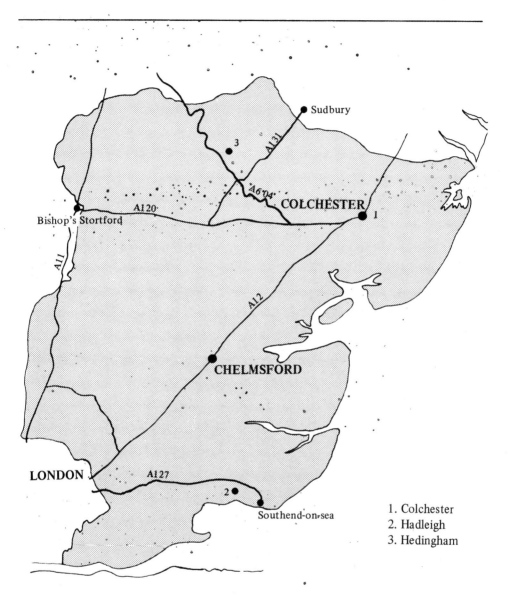

Sudbury

3

A131

A604

COLCHESTER

Bishop's Stortford

A120

A11

A12

CHELMSFORD

LONDON

A127

2

Southend-on-sea

1. Colchester
2. Hadleigh
3. Hedingham

The proud possessor of the largest surviving Keep (considerably larger than the famous White Tower, of London fame), Colchester Castle was built upon the site of a Roman Temple the foundations of which still exist within the castle itself.

Developing in the usual way from a palisade-topped mound, the castle was granted 'et turris et castellum' (both Keep and Castle) to Eudo, Steward to Henry I, as Constable of the Castle.

During the conflict between King John and the Barons, which culminated in the signing of Magna Carta, Colchester was prepared for war and when, after the document had been signed, the conflict remained unresolved, the castle was manned by French troops sent by King Philip of France to assist the Barons in their struggle.

In March, 1216, the French surrendered the Castle and it was restored to the King only to be reoccupied by the French in the following year. The Treaty of Lambeth (1217) caused the French to finally withdraw and the Castle again settled down under a fresh succession of Constables.

Colchester Castle has been used as a gaol, possibly since at least 1251, and among those held there over the years was Sir Thomas Mallory, author of the famed Morte d'Arthur. There are accounts, too, of a Trial by Battle which took place within the Castle in 1375 when John Hubert and John Bokenham fought with staves piked with horn and shields (targets) until Bokenham was overcome and, therefore, being judged guilty, was hanged.

Protestants and Catholics were both, in their turn, imprisoned at Colchester – some being burned for heresy – and a number of Royalists also enjoyed the doubtful hospitality of its dungeons. Details of these and other unsavoury events are catalogued in the illustrated guide book published by the Cultural Activities Committee of Colchester Corporation which also contains a great deal of information about the castle and its Constables through the years.

Hadleigh castle.

Below: Castle Hedingham.

HADLEIGH

This, the most important late medi-aeval castle in Essex, dates from about 1232 when it was built for Hubert de Burgh, Chief Justiciar.

Edward III had it rebuilt during the second half of the fourteenth century but much of the work has since been carried away by a landslide. The ruin is now not over impressive, particularly to those whose hopes may have been raised by its inclusion in a painting by Constable.

HEDINGHAM

The Keep at Castle Hedingham, over 100 feet high in parts, is very well preserved and has similarities with that at Rochester.

GLOUCESTERSHIRE

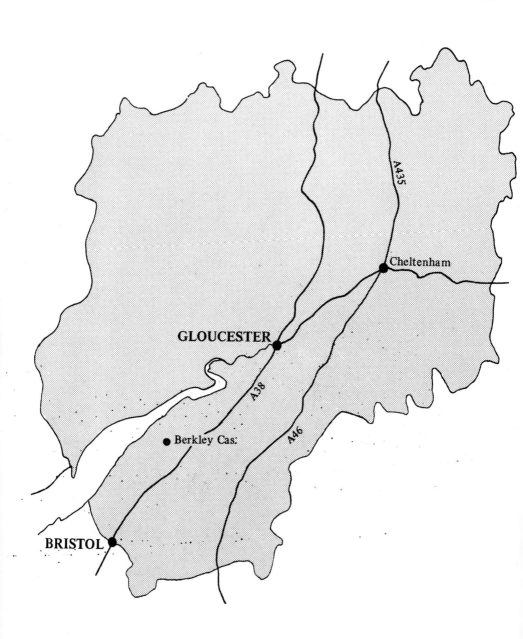

BERKELEY

Begun between 1117 and 1153, Berkeley Castle has remained ever since in the hands of the Berkeley family and is today the home of Mr. and Mrs. R. J. Berkeley.

Steeped in history, the Castle is magnificently preserved and beautifully furnished with many interesting and valuable reminders of a more leisurely age.

Here it was that King Edward II was barbarously murdered — the cell in which the deed was done being preserved and furnished and open to inspection — and here, too, the Barons of the West gathered before pressing on to Runnymede for the signing of Magna Carta by King John.

The Keep at Berkeley is interesting in that it surrounds the motte on which an earlier palisade would have stood instead of being built on top of it in the more usual manner. Other parts of the building were added, altered and enlarged by successive owners who, between them have created a massive, maze-like jumble of a building not least of whose charm is the countryside in which it is set.

HAMPSHIRE

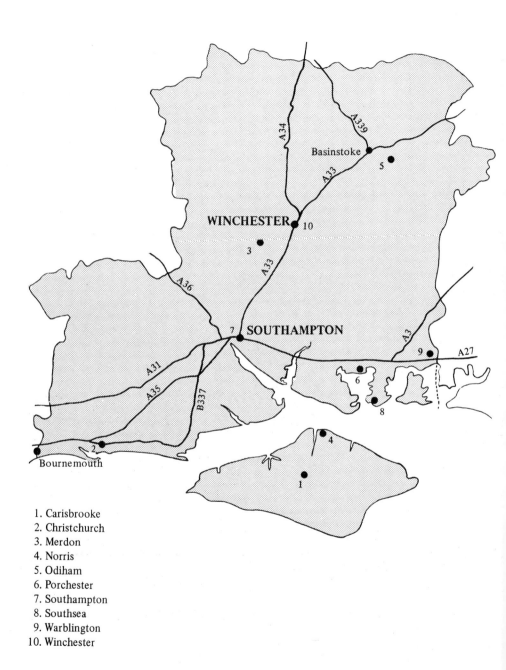

1. Carisbrooke
2. Christchurch
3. Merdon
4. Norris
5. Odiham
6. Porchester
7. Southampton
8. Southsea
9. Warblington
10. Winchester

CARISBROOKE

Slap in the middle of the Isle of Wight, Carisbrooke Castle reveals traces of Roman occupation long before the present castle was built.

Buildings here date from many periods, from the twelfth century Keep and curtain wall to the sixteenth century accommodation within the keep. An interesting feature is the treadmill positioned near the well — this would normally have been operated by a donkey though it doubtless provided exercise for the occasional pair of prisoners.

Charles I was imprisoned here for a time and Elizabeth I personally ordered the construction of certain artillery bases.

The castle contains an interesting museum illustrating its history and that of the island on which it stands.

CHRISTCHURCH

This castle, built for the Redvers family, has long since fallen away except for sections of two walls of the Keep. The substantially built Hall, however, remains and is particularly remarkable in that it is built of rough blocks of Purbeck marble.

MERDON

The few scant remains of Merdon Castle, standing as they do on a private game reserve, are not open to the public. The castle, dating from the twelfth century, was built on the site of an iron age fort, whose earthworks were probably used as part of the castle's defensive system, though the building has been criticised as having no strategic value. Slighted in 1155, the castle served for the following 300 years as a palace for the Bishops of Winchester before falling into disuse and serving as a source of stone for other buildings.

NORRIS

The stately pile of Norris Castle at East Cowes dates only from the closing years of the eighteenth century, when it was built for Lord Henry Seymour who is believed to have named it after Sir John Norris, the Elizabethan General.

Visitors may be surprised to see that the mortar used in building the house is stuck with thousands of sea shells.

ODIHAM

The fragmentary ruins of Odiham Castle date from about the beginning of the thirteenth century and, in its day, the castle seems to have been well liked by King John who is said to have visited it no fewer than twenty four times, setting out from and returning to its walls when he was called to Runnymede to set his seal on Magna Carta.

In 1216, the Castle was besieged by Louis the Dauphin, surrendering honourably after holding out for fifteen days with a garrison consisting only of three officers and ten men. Later, in 1224, the castle and manor of Odiham were granted to Princess Eleanor, sister of Henry III on her marriage to William Marshall (son of the Regent William Marshall Earl of Pembroke, q.v.) and when, after his death, Eleanor married Simon de Montfort in 1238, the castle was granted to de Montfort.

King David II of Scotland was imprisoned here from 1346 to 1357 before being ransomed for 100,000 merks (a merk was the old Scots mark, worth about 67p today) and we are told that when he was captured, King David, although severely wounded in the leg, managed to knock out most of the teeth of his captor, Sir John Copeland, Governor of Roxburgh Castle.

PORTCHESTER

This superb little mediaeval castle with its huge keep was built inside an earlier Roman/Saxon shore fort of which some sections of wall remain.

Above: Christchurch castle. Below: Porchester castle.

67

SOUTHAMPTON

Very little remains of Southampton Castle despite the fact that it was once an extremely strong and important fortress. The Bargate, however, is possibly the finest town gateway in Britain.

SOUTHSEA

This unusual, diamond shaped fort formed part of the chain of defence built by Henry VIII in the mid sixteenth century to ward off the invasion which seemed likely after he had proclaimed himself sole head of the Church in England.

Its design — angles and straight lines— represented a dramatic change in military thinking brought about by the acceptance of the gun as the weapon of the future. The fact that the fort was, with certain modifications and additions, in use from 1544 until 1960 is high tribute to the excellence of its design, though it only saw action of the type for which it was built during the summer of 1545 when the French fleet entered the Solent and sunk the Mary Rose.

In 1626, the fort was gutted by fire and remained unrepaired, despite repeated protests from a succession of commanders, for almost ten years. Eventually, however, repairs were effected and then, five years later, fire once again broke out causing extensive damage.

During the Civil War, the fort's commander declared for the King but Parliamentary forces captured it with little trouble after which it was used as a prison.

1759 saw yet another accidental disaster at Southsea when embers from a cooking fire are thought to have got at some gunpowder resulting in an explosion which wrecked the east wing.

The fort formed an important part of the sea defences maintained during the Napoleonic Wars and then, in 1814, it was enlarged and rebuilt. There being a shortage of accommodation for offenders at Portsmouth Garrison, Southsea castle was again used as a prison.

During both World Wars, the fort saw service and then, in 1960, it was acquired by Portsmouth Corporation who determined to restore it to its pre 1850 state and use it as a museum to illustrate the military history of Portsmouth.

WARBLINGTON

Another of those ruins which have been granted the courtesy title of Castle, the remains of a gatehouse at Warblington date from the sixteenth century when this was a moated house, though there is evidence to suggest that there was an earlier Manor House on the site for which a licence to crenellate was granted in about 1340.

The house was taken by the Parliamentarians during the Civil War, at about the same time as Arundel Castle (q.v.) was being besieged, and was almost certainly destroyed at that time, never to be rebuilt.

Opposite page: Dorchester castle.

WARBLINGTON
S.C.

The remains of a gatehouse at Warblington.

WINCHESTER

There are few substantial remains of
the Castle at Winchester, which was the
centre of mediaeval government and coro-
nation in England. The Great Hall which
does remain, however, is the best Mediaeval
Hall in the country after that at Westminster
and it was built as part of the general reconstruction after the Normans had taken
the castle in 1216.

For some five hundred years, Winchester remained a Royal Residence, figur-
ing prominently in the history of England
until, in the seventeenth century, it was
given by King James I to Sir Benjamin
Tichborne and his descendants.

Declaring for the King in the Civil
War, Winchester was surrendered in 1642
being again taken for the King the following
year. 1645 saw the arrival of Oliver Cromwell on a neighbouring hill from which he
bombarded the castle walls until the garrison surrendered.

The engineer who subsequently destroyed the castle was paid five pounds
for his work which included the destruction
of the entire castle with the exception of
the great hall and some subterranean passages.

70

HEREFORDSHIRE

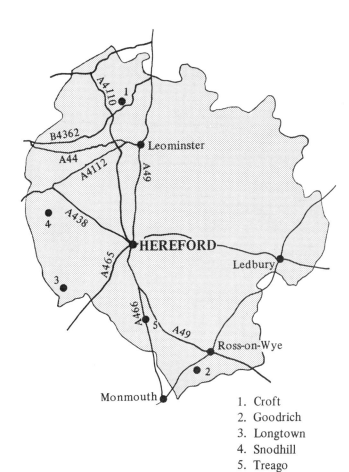

1. Croft
2. Goodrich
3. Longtown
4. Snodhill
5. Treago

Above: Croft castle.
Below: Longtown castle.

Goodrich castle.

CROFT

A National Trust property, Croft Castle dates from the fourteenth or fifteenth century originally, though it has been subject to severe modification during its long life.

The towers and outer walls of the building, of pleasant pink stone, had their windows enlarged during the sixteenth and seventeenth centuries and the interior of the building has been quite dramatically altered over the years.

LONGTOWN

Overlooking the River Monmow, the circular Keep of Longtown Castle stands ruinous and tree grown. Thought to date from the late twelfth or early thirteenth century, the castle is sadly in need of care and attention.

GOODRICH

Parts of the ruin of Goodrich Castle have a distinct air of lofty magnificence while others manage to convey a feeling of stocky solidarity.

Dating largely from the thirteenth century, the castle contains some twelfth century features, most notable of these being the Keep. It would seem, indeed, that the castle was rebuilt at least twice, for there is mention of Goodric's Castle here in 1102 but no positive indications of this have been identified on the site.

Under the care of the Department of the Environment, the castle is situated in the magnificent Herefordshire countryside not far from the Forest of Dean — an ever popular area with visitors.

Two views of Treago castle.

SNODHILL

About one mile southeast of Dorstone, Snodhill Castle is remarkable for its earthworks which encompass some ten acres of land.

The Keep, standing on a steep sided motte, dates from the early years of the thirteenth century while the Bailey walls are thought to have been built during the fourteenth century.

TREAGO

Although Treago is mentioned as early as the thirteenth century, authorities have been unable to positively date any masonry as being earlier than the late fifteenth century.

Neat and trim, the castle stands amid well manicured lawns and its present appearance owes much to alterations carried out in the seventeenth and eighteenth centuries.

HERTFORDSHIRE

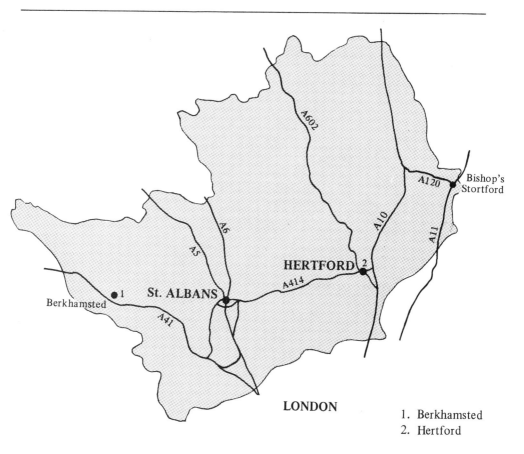

Bishop's
Stortford

HERTFORD 2

St. ALBANS

Berkhamsted 1

LONDON

1. Berkhamsted
2. Hertford

BERKHAMSTEAD

Possibly built, and certainly held, by
Robert de Mortain in the eleventh century,
Berkhamstead Castle is a fairly good
example of the Motte and Bailey type of
fortification despite its ruinous condition.

On the Motte are the lower masonry
courses of the Shell Keep and there is a
stone causeway linking the Motte with the
Bailey from which it is separated by a wet
moat.

The Curtain Wall, robbed of its
facings, is still standing almost to its original
height in places and the buildings which
stood within it are gone. At Berkhamstead
there is a second ditch outside the first,
banked on the outer side and provided with
projecting mounds from which an attacking
force could be subjected to flanking fire.

HERTFORD

Built by the Conqueror soon after 1066 to dominate the ford and the Saxon Burgh, Hertford Castle was originally a simple fortress of the Motte and Bailey type. By the time of King John (1199–1216) the governor of Hertford was Robert Fitzwalter, who was deprived of his office for being among the leaders of the barons opposing the king, and the castle had grown somewhat from the timber pallisaded structure of the previous century.

Subsequent centuries saw the castle used both as a royal palace and a royal prison, many additions being made to its fabric in order that it might prove more suitable for royal habitation. By 1608, however, the palace buildings had been demolished and a writer in Ancient Funeral Monuments of 1631 tells us that '. . . divers Princes of this land have often made their residence in this Towne; by which means it hath beene in former times of great state, estimation and beautie, but now for want of that generall convention, the Castle is greatly decayed, these Parish Churches much ruined, and the Towne neither greatly inhabited nor much frequented.'

Although the palace buildings were gone, some sections of the castle were still habitable and it was around these that other buildings were erected, notably during the seventeenth and eighteenth centuries. The nineteenth century saw the castle used for purposes as varied as a teaching college, a dispensary for free medicine for the poor and as lodgings for visiting Assize judges.

Since 1911, the castle has been leased to Hertford Borough Council who found that, by 1936, it offered insufficient space for the number of offices it contained. Accordingly, additions and alterations were made to the building during the course of which some original mediaeval ceilings were discovered.

HUNTINGDON

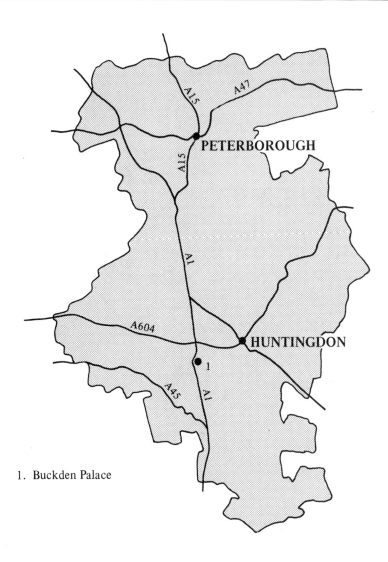

1. Buckden Palace

BUCKDEN PALACE

A Palace of the Bishops of Lincoln, Buckden was twice rebuilt, once in the thirteenth and again in the fifteenth century, and most of the brick palace that we see today dates from the second rebuilding which was started by Bishop Rotherham (made Archbishop of York in 1480) and continued by his successors, Bishop John Russell and Bishop William Smith, one of the founders of Brasenose College, Oxford.

In 1592, during the great wave of witch hunting which swept the country, the Witches of Warboys — John Samwell with his wife, Alice and daughter, Agnes — were here accused of dealings with the devil and, found guilty by Bishop Wickham,

were hanged the following year.

During the Civil War, Buckden passed into secular hands, being returned to the clergy at the Restoration of the Monarchy in 1660 when repairs were carried out to put right the damage sustained during the Parliamentary period. By the nineteenth century, the importance of the Palace had waned and an amount of demolition work was carried out, furniture and building materials being sold at auction.

Now in the possession of the Claretians, a Congregation of Missionaries, Buckden is tended and preserved in the Faith in which it was built so long ago.

KENT

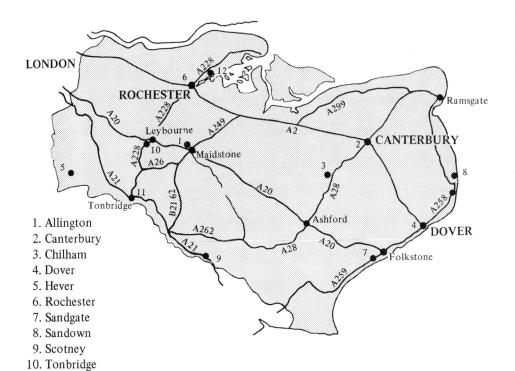

ALLINGTON

This charming castle, dating from 1282, was built by Stephen of Penchester, Warden of the Cinque Ports and Constable of Dover Castle under Edward I. Never intended as a purely military stronghold, the castle has more the character of a large and well fortified manor house than a barracks, a peaceful impression which is heightened by the community of Carmelite Monks (Whitefriars) who now own Allington. The presence of Carmelites here is nicely ironic; during the Dissolution of the Monasteries under Henry VIII, the then owner of Allington was Sir Thomas Wyatt who received the Abbeys of Malling and Boxley as well as the Carmelite Priory at Aylesford, pulling down the church belonging to the latter establishment and selling the stone.

Sometime later, the Wyatt family fell into disfavour and emigrated to Virginia where they re-established their fortunes. Many of their American descendants now visit the old family home at regular intervals.

Beside being open to visitors in the usual way, Allington serves as a retreat house and Christian Conference Centre —

possibly the ideal use for such a building and one which ensures its continued life in a gracious and eminently worthwhile manner.

Built by the Conqueror, the Keep of Canterbury Castle stands within the ancient city, the old Roman Wall forming one side of its Bailey.

Isolated and ruinous, the Keep is all that now remains of the castle and its design suggests that it dates from about 1080.

CHILHAM

Close by the fine Jacobean mansion stands the Norman Keep of Chilham Castle, built by Bishop Odo of Bayeux, an illigitimate half brother of the Conqueror, on the site of earlier Roman and Saxon fortifications.

The home of Viscount Massereene and Ferrard, Chilham Castle stands close to the junction of the A252 with the A28 and is clearly signposted. There is a nature trail, almost 35 acres of Capability Brown gardens, falconry and free flying eagle displays, a cafeteria and a wildlife section. The Norman Keep and the Jacobean mansion, however, are not open to visitors, although banquets are held in the Keep.

One of the first features to be seen from the cross channel ferry as it steams towards Dover Harbour, Dover Castle stands high on the cliffs above the town.

Here it was that the Romans built a lighthouse whose remains can still be seen within the castle walls. Here, too, William, another conqueror, came to have the Castle surrendered to him by the ill fated Harold.

It was Henry II who established Dover as a massive, stonebuilt castle, spending some £7,000 on its construction at a time when the total Crown income was something under £10,000 per year. The castle's plan was greatly influenced by experience gained on the Crusades and was a unique departure from the established Western pattern of defensive building of the time.

The present building owes its appearance to the work of numerous builders over the centuries, each adding a feature and strengthening others as armaments and the methods of warfare changed to make fresh demands on the castle's defences. So important a military site has Dover been that a garrison has been stationed here continuously until 1958.

Chilham Castle.   *Opposite page: Dover castle.*

Hever Castle began life as a thirteenth century fortified Manor House within the safety of whose walls the Bullen (Boleyn) family built their Tudor house some two hundred years later. After the death of Anne Boleyn's father in 1538, Henry VIII took possession of the castle, granting it to Anne of Cleves, his divorced fourth wife. Little further of note occurred here for many years until, in 1903, the property was bought by William Waldorf Astor (later First Viscount Astor of Hever Castle) who carried out a mammoth programme of restoration and rebuilding, restoring the interior of the house and adding the Tudor-style village which stands beyond the moat.

Although much of the 'mediaeval' decoration of Hever is of twentieth century origin, the overall impression gained is one of graciousness and the quality of the work is high enough to ensure that it escapes the pitfall of phoniness into which some castle restorers have fallen so sadly.

The magnificent gardens contain some superb pieces of statuary (and a collection of interesting sculpted columns, sarcophagi, and Pompeian storage jars) and the interior of the castle abounds with other works of art, many of which commemorate Hever's connection with Henry VIII and all of which are carefully documented in the well produced souvenir guide book.

Rochester castle

ROCHESTER

The twelfth century Keep of Rochester Castle, standing on the right bank of the River Medway, is one of the biggest and best of its kind ro have survived the passage of centuries.

Two notable sieges punctuate the castle's history — the first and greatest was mounted for almost three months by King John against whom the garrison held out until, having eaten their horses, they were starved into capitulating. The second, and unsuccessful, besieger was Simon de Montfort.

An interesting feature at Rochester is the central well with all floors built in such a way as to allow water to be drawn at every level instead of just the basement as was more commonly the practice.

SANDGATE

Another of the Henrician coastal defence forts, Sandgate Castle was drastically altered in 1806, when the central section was converted into a gun fort more suitable to the weapons of the nineteenth century than those of 1539, the year of the castle's origin.

SANDOWN CASTLE, DEAL

One of three local Henrician forts, Sandown Castle suffered greatly as a result of storms.

Barely anything remains of the fort now, although the local Council have placed a seat on the knob of stonework which can still be seen.

SCOTNEY

Closed to members of the public, Scotney Castle is an attractive building consisting of a section of a fourteenth century castle to which has been added a seventeenth century house.

During the nineteenth century, part of the house was pulled down in an effort to make the building even more picturesque when viewed across a shrub filled quarry from the new house built on the nearby hill.

ST. LEONARD'S TOWER

This small, ragged topped Norman tower, standing on a rocky shelf, is believed to have been built around 1100.

The inside contains evidence to suggest that it had two floors, the lower of which was only about five feet above ground level.

TONBRIDGE

The massive Keep-Gatehouse at Tonbridge is interesting in that it illustrates the ultimate in this particular development of castle design.

Every entrance and exit of this stout building was equipped with a portcullis — even those leading to the wall walks — in order that the Lord might remain as secure against a rebellion from within his own garrison as against the onslaughts of external foes. Such an arrangement was undoubtedly excellent as far as it went but it must have proved inconvenient from the point of view of domestic comfort, with drawbridge and portcullis winding gear cropping up all over the Lord's private quarters.

Scotney castle.

Above: St. Leonards tower at West Malling. Below: Tonbridge castle.

UPNOR

Built to protect the Dockyards at Chatham, this is one of the few Henrician forts which is not based on a geometric pattern.

Added to and improved on the landward side by Arthur Gregory between 1599 and 1601, the castle failed the supreme test when the Dutch fleet sailed up the Medway to Upnor and set fire to the English fleet.

WALMER

Private residence of Lord Walmer, this Castle is only open to the public at certain times.

One of three castles built locally for Henry VIII to cover shipping in the Downland area, this fortress is another of the geometric essays which are to be found all along the South Coast. (see section on Henrician Forts).

Upnor castle.

Walmer castle.

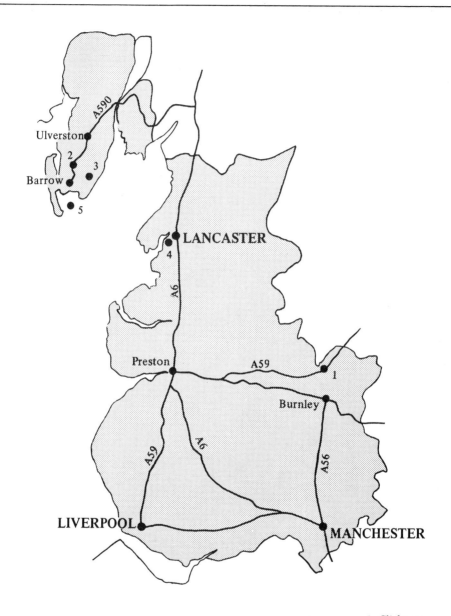

1. Clitheroe
2. Dalton
3. Gleaston
4. Lancaster
5. Piel tower

The small Keep of Clitheroe Castle, owned by the Borough of Clitheroe, is believed to date from about 1086 when it was built for Roger de Poitou, the first Norman Lord of the Honour of Clitheroe.

The naturally defensible site was already occupied by a Saxon community, under Orme the Englishman, who had established a township of approximately the same size of Clitheroe as it is today and, with the coming of the Normans, it was not long before the timber palisades and Thane's hall were removed to make way for the limestone building of the Norman Lord.

The small size of the castle was dictated by the contours of the ground on which it was built and, although the Gatehouse and other buildings have gone or have been replaced (to some extent following slighting after the Civil War), the area retains a certain magic which the presence of Local Authority Offices fails to dispel.

The view from the top of the Keep is superb, taking in the whole of Clitheroe and the entire Ribble Valley, and there is an interestingly small museum in the grounds which is open on three afternoons per week from May to September (Tuesdays, Thursdays and Saturdays).

DALTON TOWER

Called Dalton Tower locally, this small tower dates from the fourteenth century, and was probably one of a number of towers built as a result of the Scottish raids which continued throughout the first half of that century.

It has served its time as a courthouse and gaol and has several times during its lifetime fallen into decay and been repaired. Now, however, it is the property of the National Trust in whose hands it is likely to enjoy a degree of security in retirement.

Dalton Tower.

Lancaster castle.

GLEASTON

Tucked away in a valley and by-passed by most traffic, the ruins of Gleaston Castle date mainly from the fourteenth century when the castle walls doubtless proved a necessary defence against the ravages of marauding bands of Scottish raiders. In fact there is evidence to suggest that the structure was both strengthened and enlarged after a raid by Robert the Bruce in 1318.

The fifteenth century saw the building's finest days, the Baronial block being improved and pleasure gardens created by William, Fifth Baron Harrington, but, as so often happened, he died leaving no male heir and the castle fell into disrepair after 1457. By 1530 the castle was reported as being in ruins by Leyland, who in his 'Itinerary' wrote 'There is a ruine and waulles of a castell in Lancastershire, cawlyed Gleston Castell, sometime longyneth to the Lorde Harrington ...' though it must be remembered that chroniclers of that period were inclined to overemphasise the ruinous aspects of buildings.

LANCASTER

Lancaster Castle, one time possession of John of Gaunt, stands rather drably in a town noted for its linoleum.

The Keep, dating from 1090, was damaged by Robert the Bruce in 1322. John of Gaunt repaired it and one of the turrets is still known as John of Gaunt's Chair.

Parts of the Castle are used as law courts and prison cells while others are more generally open to the public. There is a display of prison equipment in Hadrian's Tower.

Piel Castle, called of old the Pile of Fouldrey, stands on a small, water encircled knob of rock near the south end of the Isle of Walney.

King Stephen (1135–1154) granted certain lands to the then Abbot of Furness on condition that he 'build, sustain and garrison' a castle here 'for a Defence of the Country'. Piel castle was the result of this agreement but we are told that, by the time of Henry I, the castle had fallen into such a state of disrepair that it was confiscated by the Crown, only later being returned to the Abbey on the firm assurance that it would be put in good order again.

When, after the Wars of the Roses, Lambert Simnel was claimed as the son of the murdered Duke of Clarence, his supporters gathered on Piel Island along with a force of 2,000 Flemish and great numbers of Irish soldiers — a total of close on 8,000 men. They took possession of the undefended castle and it was from here that they set out to march southward to defeat at Stokefield, near Newark. This was the last foreign invasion of England.

Now in a ruinous state, the building is the property of Barrow in Furness Corporation.

LEICESTERSHIRE

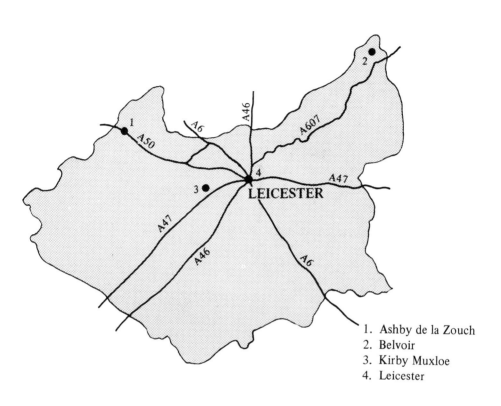

1. Ashby de la Zouch
2. Belvoir
3. Kirby Muxloe
4. Leicester

ASHBY DE LA ZOUCHE

Close by the church, in the centre of the town, the ruins of Ashby Castle are fairly large and palely impressive.

Given by Edward IV to his Chancellor and fellow Yorkist, William, Lord Hastings, the original manor house had belonged to the Earl of Ormonde, a Lancastrian. Hastings converted the house into a small castle with a fantastic Keep cum Tower House which was doubtless considered necessary by so prominent a man in the latter half of the troubled fifteenth century. It did not save him from the headsman's axe, however, for he was beheaded by Richard III in 1483.

During the Civil War, Henry Hastings, a second son of the fifth Earl of Huntingdon, led the Royalist troops in Leicestershire, defending Ashby Castle for almost two years against the Parliament. The building proved too strong to be taken by storm and the garrison eventually made an honourable surrender after suffering from starvation and an attack of the plague. The castle was slighted by Parliament following its capture and its life seems to have ended at that time.

BELVOIR

This is one of the extensively rebuilt castles whose present appearance is so imposing thanks to the romanticism of the eighteenth and nineteenth centuries.

A treasure house of military souvenirs and works of art of all kinds from painted ceilings to marble fireplaces, Belvoir fits well into the 'stately home' category.

The first castle built on the site was raised by Robert de Todeni, standard bearer to William the Conqueror, and his coffin, found in the eighteenth century, can be seen in the present castle.

Destroyed during the Wars of the Roses, Belvoir remained ruinous for over fifty years before being rebuilt by Thomas, First Earl of Rutland, work continuing for almost thirty two years.

The Civil War saw the rebuilt Belvoir besieged by the Parliament's forces for four months before the garrison surrendered with honour; as usual, the castle was the subject of a demolition order. Within five years, however, the walls were again rising under the direction of John Webb, at that time a pupil of Inigo Jones, and work on the castle and gardens was completed in 1668.

Toward the end of the eighteenth century, more alterations to the castle were considered but not carried out until early in the nineteenth century when, the work largely completed, fire broke out causing tremendous damage. The present building dates extensively from the final rebuilding after the fire.

Close to the M1, the remains of this brick built castle stand with shaky elegance among the not too good surroundings.

The moat is crisp and square, the lawns smooth trimmed and the brickwork warm, all contributing to an atmosphere of calm graciousness which has much in common with the Castle of Ashby de la Zouche, (q.v.). Both castles were built by Lord Hastings, one of the most powerful men of his day and one whose death as a traitor is well known to all who are conversant with Shakespeare's Richard III.

Kirby Muxloe castle.

Visitors to Leicester may be forgiven if they fail to find the Castle; a pair of small Gatehouses, Dungeons and a trace of timbered ceiling in the Courthouse is all that remains of John of Gaunt's once important castle.

Thought to have been established in 1068, the castle began its life as a typical Motte and Bailey castle of earthworks and wooden palisades. Building in stone is believed to have been started by Robert de Beaumont during the first half of the twelfth century.

Simon de Montfort succeeded to Leicester for a time but, on his death in 1265, the castle was granted to the King's son, Edmund Crouchback who, with his successors, held a vast conglomeration of castles and lands all over the country which later comprised the Duchy of Lancaster.

It was during the time of John of Gaunt that the castle saw its greatest days, the extravagance of the hospitality rivalling that of the king's own household. After John of Gaunt's death the castle fell into a steady decline from which it never recovered, the last authenticated date of its occupation being 1483, when Richard III wrote a letter 'from my Castle of Leicester'. Charles I sold parts of the castle, which had become ruined, to raise funds (see also Lincoln) and, during the Civil War, its hastily improvised defences fell easily to the forces of the Crown and again to the Parliamentarians.

LINCOLNSHIRE

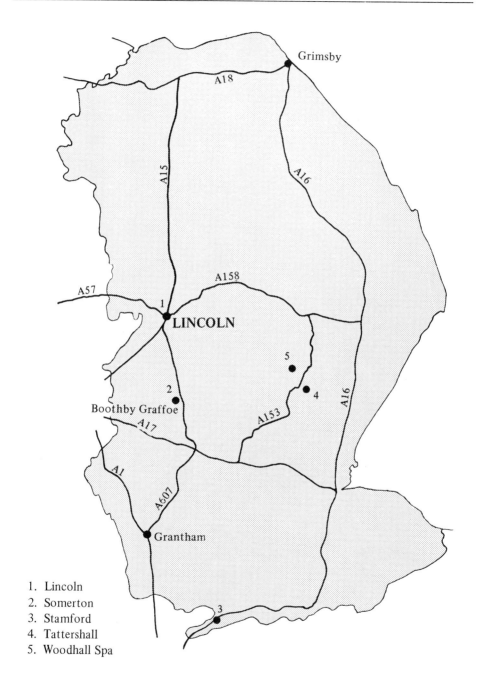

Grimsby

A18

A15

A16

A57

A158

1 **LINCOLN**

5

2
Boothby Graffoe

A153

4

A16

A17

A1

A607

Grantham

3

1. Lincoln
2. Somerton
3. Stamford
4. Tattershall
5. Woodhall Spa

LINCOLN

For a castle of this size (the walls enclose six and a quarter acres) there is surprisingly little to see: largely as a result of its having been used as a gaol, ugly Victorian prison buildings abound within the walls.

An unusual feature is the existence of two Keeps. One, now known as the Observatory Tower, takes its name from the nineteenth century turret built on its summit by a past Governor of the Gaol who was a keen student of astronomy. The other, the Lucy Tower, is a circular Shell Keep, open to the sky with trees growing inside it. Beneath the trees are rows of shabby gravestones marking the resting places of prisoners who died (or were executed) here in the days when the castle was used as a gaol.

The erection of the castle was ordered by the Conqueror in 1068, on a site earlier occupied by the Romans, and, although its first half century of life seems to have passed fairly peacefully, it soon became the scene of a power struggle between rivals for the office of Sheriff of Lincolnshire.

Later, when French forces arrived in England at the invitation of the Barons, they took Lincoln, soon to flee before the approaching army of King John. The castle was taken a second time by the baronial forces who were again routed by Royalists under William Marshall, who pillaged the city.

The Civil Wars saw Lincoln once more embroiled in troubles which resulted from the castle changing hands several times; a process doubtless made easier by the fact that Charles I had earlier sold some of the castle's defensive ditches as a means of raising money without having recourse to Parliament.

Somerton

SOMERTON

Built by Anthony Bek — later Bishop Bek of Durham — Somerton Castle was granted its licence to crenellate in 1281.

It was here that King John of France was held to ransom after his capture at Poitiers by the Black Prince in 1356. Established here with his son, Prince Philip, and his household, the King seems to have spent some seven months of comfortable living at Somerton, renting a cellar in Boston for his wine, entertaining the local gentry and even distributing alms and gifts to the Vicar of Boothby at Christmas, Epiphany and Candlemas. Rumours of an impending French invasion caused the decision to remove the King to the greater safety of Berkhampstead.

Now incorporated in a farmhouse, little remains of the original castle apart from a couple of towers and a few sections of wall.

STAMFORD

It was inevitable that, somewhere, a castle should have fallen to the power of the motor car. At Stamford, the old castle has been levelled to make a car park. A few sections of wall remain here and there, with postern gates by King's Mill Lane and Bath Row.

TATTERSHALL

Bought by the late Marquess Curzon of Kedleston K.G. in 1911, Tattershall Castle was partially restored by him after it had stood empty for over 200 years.

Now administered by the National Trust, the brick built Great Tower is open to the public; each floor, replaced and accessible, having a descriptive note affixed to the wall as an aid to visitors who like to understand the layout and use of the various rooms.

Most of the castle buildings have gone now but the great size of the brick built Tower rising from neat lawns and reed filled moats, and the nearby huge Collegiate Church of the Holy Trinity, dwarf the houses of the small village in which they stand.

TOWER ON THE MOOR

About a mile and a half from the centre of Woodhall Spa stands a gaunt finger of brickwork – all that is left of the Tower on the Moor built by the Cromwells of Tattershall (q.v.).

Smaller than the Great Tower of Tattershall Castle, and of a somewhat later date, this ruin stands among scrubby trees and coarse grasses overlooking Woodhall Spa Golf Course.

LONDON

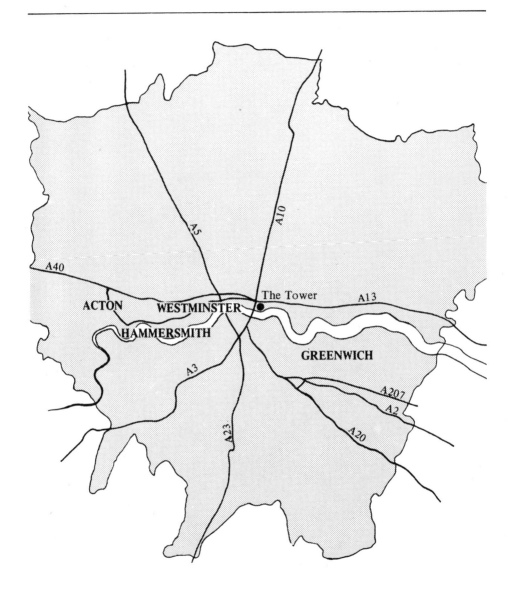

THE TOWER OF LONDON

The Tower of London was begun by William the Conqueror as a means of protecting and controlling the city of London.

The only remaining building from that period is the White Tower, which is one of the oldest and largest surviving Keeps in western Europe, a massively strong and uncomfortable building which was clearly designed for no other purpose than that of security. During the Middle Ages, this Tower was whitewashed — the practice which doubtless gave it its name — and we are told that, in 1241, King Henry III also had the interior of the Royal Apartments white-

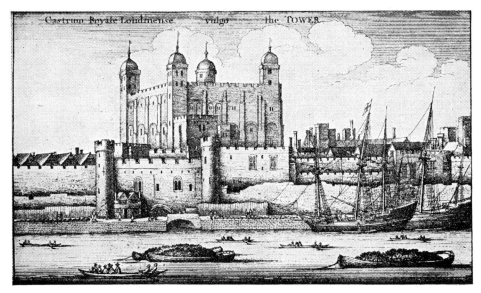

The Tower of London - engraved by Hollar

washed beside ordering the Chapel to be decorated with paintings and stained glass.

In its time, the Tower has served as a fortress, a palace and a prison beside having housed the Public Records, the Royal Mint, the Crown Jewels and the Royal Menagerie. Naturally enough, in the nine centuries which have passed since its first building, the Tower has been extended and altered considerably until, now, the area contained within the moat covers some eighteen acres.

Although it bristles with historic armaments and martial pageantry, the Tower of London is now a great and beautiful museum containing many of the treasures and traditions of the greatest and most shameful days of British history.

NORFOLK

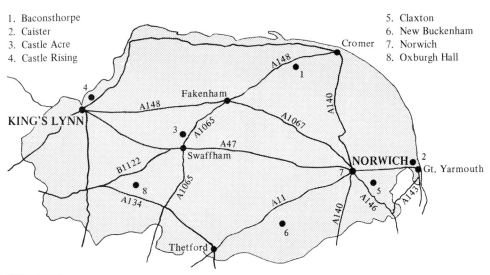

Caister

BACONSTHORPE

Built between the years of 1450 and 1486, the castle at Baconsthorpe dates from about the same time as that at Kirby Muxloe in Leicestershire.

Extremely ruinous, the castle consists of sections of flint built wall punctuated with fragmentary Towers dominated by the Gatehouse — a ruined shell with knapped flints.

CAISTER

The ruin of Caister Castle houses a motor museum.

The castle was built by Sir John Fastolfe, accepted as the model for Shakespeare's Falstaff (though the guide book is at great pains to point out that Shakespeare's characterisation is 'a cruel and unfair defamation of his true character, written many years after his death'), probably during the early years of the fifteenth century.

Well defended by encircling moats and walls, the castle lacks the strictly military appearance that would not have been out of place at the time of its buildings, great attention obviously having been paid to domestic comfort for the inhabitants.

After the death of Sir John, the castle was claimed by the Duke of Norfolk who, after years of legal proceedings, eventually delivered an ultimatum and proceeded to take the castle by force of arms. By the final year of the sixteenth century, Caister Castle was empty and it soon fell into ruins.

NEW BUCKENHAM

Having given Old Buckenham Castle to the Augustinians, William II de Albini set about building himself a new castle.

Dating from the mid twelfth century, the castle was altered and turned round during the following century by means of the building of a large Gatehouse to the west.

The Keep is of particular interest, being built to a circular plan some time before these became generally known in England.

NORWICH

Although Norwich Castle, as a fortification, dates from shortly after the Conquest, the Keep was not built until almost one hundred years afterwards.

Refaced in Bath stone by Salvin in the eighteen thirties, this great building (almost as large as the White Tower) looks sadly false despite the accuracy of the

work which clearly shows the type of decorative arcading which is to be found in its unrestored state at Castle Rising.

This great Keep, the only mediaeval building remaining in the Inner Bailey, is now used as a museum.

OXBURGH HALL

Built on the edge of the Fens by Sir Edmund Bedingfield after the granting of a licence in 1482, this fine, moated, fortified house was subjected to having its Hall range demolished at the end of the eighteenth century. This was rebuilt about sixty years later in a style which, though not strictly correct, is undeniably attractive.

The chief surviving building from the fifteenth century is the great Gatehouse, brick built and the most prominent of its type and period.

Castle Acre Priory

CASTLE ACRE

Covering a total area of some fifteen acres, this has been authoritatively described as one of the grandest Motte and Bailey castles of England.

Standing on a wild and tree grown site, the castle remains are fragmentary and spiky, the Keep having been reduced to its foundations within the encircling wall of the Shell Keep.

CASTLE RISING

The earthworks surrounding Castle Rising extend for some twelve acres with a main Ditch of almost 60 feet depth and a Rampart over 60 feet high.

Dating from the middle of the twelfth century, the castle is similar in style to that at Norwich, particularly with regard to the Keeps which are of the Hall, as opposed to the Tower, type. The Keep here is one of the largest in England and it is extensively decorated with arcading while its corner turrets and buttresses are enriched with vertical roll moulding.

This fine castle was built by William de Albini, later Earl of Sussex, and had the relatively short lifespan of only three centuries before it was reported as being in ruins.

CLAXTON

The long, red brick wall that remains of this fifteenth century castle stands comfortably beside the nineteenth century frontage of the seventeenth century house which now bears its name.

NORTHAMPTONSHIRE

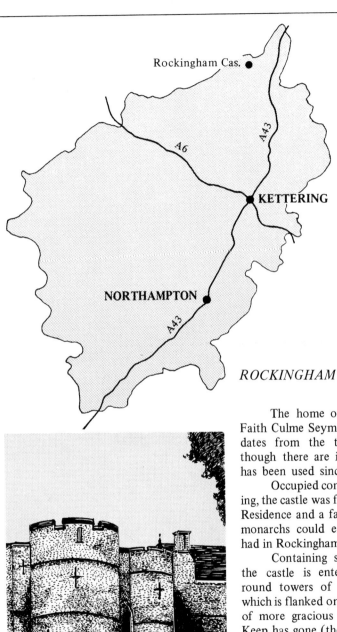

Rockingham Cas. ●

A43

A6

● KETTERING

NORTHAMPTON ●

A43

ROCKINGHAM

The home of Sir Michael and Lady Faith Culme Seymour, Rockingham Castle dates from the time of the Conqueror, though there are indications that the site has been used since pre Roman times.

Occupied continuously since its building, the castle was for five centuries a Royal Residence and a favourite spot from which monarchs could enjoy the hunting to be had in Rockingham Forest.

Containing something for everyone, the castle is entered between the squat round towers of the Norman Gatehouse which is flanked on either side by the backs of more gracious buildings. The Norman Keep has gone (there is now a rose garden in its place) as have most of the other original buildings and the greater part of the castle as we see it today is of Tudor origin; very beautiful and very peaceful in its rural setting.

NORTHUMBERLAND

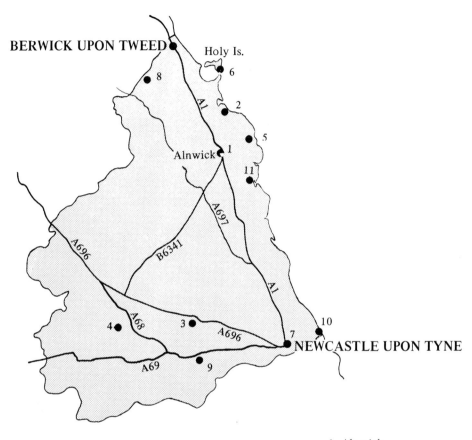

BERWICK UPON TWEED

Holy Is.

8

6

2

A1

5

Alnwick 1

11

A697

A696

B6341

A1

4

A68

3

A696

7 **NEWCASTLE UPON TYNE**

10

A69

9

1. Alnwick
2. Bamburgh
3. Belsay
4. Chipchase
5. Dunstanburgh
6. Lindisfarne
7. Newcastle
8. Norham
9. Prudhoe
10. Tynemouth
11. Warkworth

109

ALNWICK

Alnwick Castle is one of those large, rambling structures which seem to suggest centuries of purely random additions to the original buildings.

Beginning as a standard Motte and Bailey type castle, a Shell Keep was the first stone building to rise from the site during the twelfth century. Every subsequent period left marks of its passing on the plan of Alnwick and, although it was a neglected ruin for the two hundred years following the Border Wars, it was restored during the eighteenth and nineteenth centuries by the Dukes of Northumberland.

BAMBURGH

This is another of those vast, majestic castles which owes its present appearance to the architectural aspirations of its tenants over many generations.

Site of the seat of the Kings of Northumbria, Bamburgh was the scene of considerable resistance to the early Norman Kings first by the English Earls of Northumberland and then by the Scots, who captured it during the reign of Stephen and lost it again to his successor, Henry II. Henry III ordered the building of a great 'grange' and other works whose completion marked the high point in the castle's development.

Naturally enough, Bamburgh figured regularly in the wars waged against and by the Scots and, despite the general increase of expenditure on castles, it suffered considerably during the late thirteenth and early fourteenth centuries from lack of maintenance and the weather. Restored to strength, the castle played a prominent part in the Wars of the Roses before being ruinously damaged by gunfire — the first English castle to succumb to this new development in the art of warfare.

The years that followed saw Banburgh slowly restored and rebuilt until a new

Bamburgh Castle.

impetus was given to the work by Doctor John Sharp, Archdeacon of Northumberland, who, during the second half of the eighteenth century, set up a hospital and a dispensary within its walls, beside establishing a school here for the children of the poor and adding a library which was available to the public free of charge.

In 1894, the castle was sold to the First Lord Armstrong who carried out extensive further building work which has been criticised by those who would prefer to have seen the building left an historic ruin. This work was completed in 1903 and the castle is now partly inhabited and partly open to the public — an eminently sensible arrangement.

BELSAY

An oblong tower, one of the largest in the country, with short wings adjoining the northwest and southwest ends; that is

Belsay Castle as it was until a house was added in the seventeenth century.

Belsay Castle.

CHIPCHASE TOWER

The stoutly built, fourteenth century Tower at Chipchase stands rather bleak and forlorn looking despite the addition of a seventeenth century Manor House and the suggestion that there might have been an earlier, mediaeval manor on the same site.

DUNSTANBURGH

Standing atop one hundred foot high cliffs, the ruin of Dunstanburgh Castle has been steadily decaying since the sixteenth century.

Built in the early fourteenth century by the Earl of Lancaster, the castle was the largest in the country encompassing eleven acres within its walls. It was of great strategic importance during the wars with the Scots since it guarded a harbour which, Berwick falling regularly into Scottish hands, was essential for the supply of the English forces in the area.

LINDISFARNE

The small, sixteenth century castle standing on Lindisfarne (or Holy Island) looks, from the air, curiously like a stone built ship cast up on dry land and converted to a dwelling house.

Built to defend the harbour in preparation for Lord Hertford's expedition against the Scots, the castle was constructed of stone from the island's recently dissolved Monastery and originally consisted of a series of blockhouses and bulwarks. Its military significance ceased with the union of Scotland and England and, although it was garrisoned during the Civil War, the castle saw little action, its function degenerating into that of a Coastguard Station until, at the beginning of this century, it was restored by Sir Edward Luytens. In 1944, the castle became the property of the National Trust and the flag which flies from its pole indicates that it is open to the public.

Although Lindisfarne may be reached by road when the tide is out, the causeway should never be crossed at any time there is water on it.

The remote setting of Dunstanburgh Castle.

Above: Chipchase Castle. Below: Lindisfarne Castle on Holy Island.

Considering the importance of Newcastle as a crossing place for the River Tyne, it is not surprising that both Romans and Normans built fortifications here.

The first Norman castle was doubtless of the standard timber walled type which was not replaced by the stone building we see today until the time of King Henry II who had regained Northumberland from the Scots.

The Civil War saw Newcastle held for the Royalists for a time and the castle, we are told, held out three days longer than the town against the roundheads. After the Civil War, the castle was used, like so many of its kind, as a gaol and then, toward the end of the eighteenth century, the Keep was advertised to let, the suggestion being that it would convert suitably into a windmill.

Nowadays the Keep, grimy and rather squalid looking, houses a museum and glowers impotently at the trains which rumble past on the line dividing the castle precinct into two parts.

Above: The Keep at Newcastle.

Below: The ruins of Norham castle.

114

Prudhoe Castle.

NORHAM

For a splendidly stirring description of Norham Castle there can be no better source than the first canto of Marmion.

Built in the twelfth century to guard a fording place of the Tweed, this blocky, rugged castle figured prominently in the dealings between Scots and English before the two countries were united under a single crown. Much damage was done to the walls by the dreaded Mons Meg — the great cannon cast at Mons — which James IV of Scotland used to batter the barbican from a site which is still to be seen on the Scottish side of the Tweed.

Since 1923, Norham has been in the care of the Commissioners of H.M. Works and the various successors of that department who have carried out considerable excavation and restorative work on the site.

PRUDHOE

The superb ruin of Prudhoe Castle stands some quarter of a mile to the north of the town.

Built during the reign of Henry II to replace an earlier earthwork, the castle was begun by Odinel II de Umfraville who was responsible for the Keep and a curtain wall. Later builders strengthened the original work and, in the usual way, added extra fortifications and chambers as they saw fit or as the King directed.

Odinel II was something of a thorn in the paw of the Scottish King William the Lion and Prudhoe was twice attacked by that royal personage who was determined that Odinel should pay the price for refusing to acknowledge his hereditary right to the county of Northumberland. Both attacks failed to achieve their objective and, when the king was captured at Alnwick, Odinel was one of the knights who took him.

Passing into the hands of the Percy family — Earls and Dukes of Northumberland — in the fourteenth century, Prudhoe seems to have been neglected, for, by the mid sixteenth century, it was described as being a ruin.

Tynemouth Castle was built to protect the Priory whose ruin shares the same rocky promontory overlooking the mouth of the river.

Smooth lawned and mellow stoned, the ruins of both buildings exude an aura of restful antiquity, the castle dating from the thirteenth and fourteenth centuries, and provide a pleasant spot in which to spend a few sunny hours.

During the Civil War, the castle was held for the king for a year before the Parliamentarians turned their attentions upon it and captured it. Held for the Parliament by Colonel Lilburn, the castle was soon a Royalist fortress again following the Colonel's change of allegiance — a mistake which caused his head to be cut off and displayed on a pike from the castle walls.

Later converted to be a private residence, the castle is now under the care of the Department of the Environment and has been returned to a state of properly tended decay.

The huge remains of the late fourteenth century Keep of Warkworth, stronghold of the Percys, is one of the most impressive examples of the architecture of its day and is a remarkable illustration of the way in which mediaeval builders combined the elements of military security and domestic convenience in a single structure.

The first stone buildings at Warkworth were put up by Henry, a son of David I of Scotland, on a site that was probably occupied by a great house of Saxon times. When Northumberland was regained by the English Crown, Henry II gave the castle to Roger Fitz Richard whose descendants held it for almost two hundred years before it passed to the Percy family.

Although the castle is largely a magnificent ruin, the Duke of Northumberland retains a private suite of rooms on the second floor of the Keep for use during his visits to Warkworth.

Tynemouth Castle, thirteenth century.

Two views of Warkworth castle.

NOTTINGHAMSHIRE

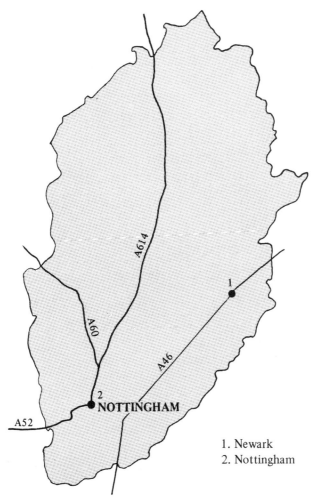

1. Newark
2. Nottingham

Nottingham Castle.

NEWARK

Situated above the River Trent, the remains of this once-magnificent castle now provide a backdrop for municipal flower beds and lawns whose peace and fragrance are subject to shattering interruptions from the nearby cattle market.

The Roman Road (Fosse Way) from Leicester to Lincoln was diverted to the east by Alexander, Bishop of Lincoln, in about 1130 in order that he might build his castle close by the ford across the River Trent. Using his fishpond as a moat and building a rampart for the defence of the castle, the Bishop was permitted to employ one third of his soldiers to do Castle Guard and to build a bridge across the river.

On this site, a second castle was built toward the end of the twelfth century whose walls enclosed an area of about five thousand square feet. All that remains of this building is the West Tower, the Main Gate and some sections of walling. It was in this castle that King John died in 1216.

Two years after the death of King John, the castle was besieged and badly battered by missiles cast from 'great engines', and there is evidence to suggest that what amounted almost to a third castle was built following the destruction caused at that time.

The destruction of the castle followed its defence in the Royalist cause during the Civil War and it was never rebuilt.

119

The 'rather benign looking ducal mansion' that is Nottingham Castle today can be nothing but a disappointment to those who were brought up with tales of Robin Hood and the villainous Sheriff of Nottingham.

The earliest origins of Nottingham are obscure but it is certain that a timber castle was constructed on the Rock about two years after the Battle of Hastings, being gradually replaced by stone buildings and walls as time went by.

Nottingham has figured in almost every period of trouble in Britain from that time onward. Stephen and Matilda fought over it as did King John and his brother, Richard I. Mortimer was captured here by Edward III, to be taken to Tyburn and hanged, drawn and quartered on the common gallows.

For some two hundred years, if all the legends are to be believed, Robin Hood and his band of outlaws made merry in and around Nottingham (a verifiable Robin Hood does actually appear on the scene during the fourteenth century and Edward III is said to have recruited many archers from the poachers in Sherwood Forest when he defeated the Scots at Halidon Hill). Owain Glyndwr, the Welshman, was imprisoned here for a time as were many captives brought from France by Henry V. The castle saw service in the Yorkist cause during the Wars of the Roses and was the scene (despite its by now ruinous condition) of Charles's attempt to rally support at the start of the Civil War. Not spectacularly successful, he moved away to Shrewsbury and the castle was garrisoned for Parliament under whose flag it was several times unsuccessfully attacked and eventually pulled down when hostilities ceased.

Nottingham Castle as it would have appeared in the seventeenth century.

OXFORDSHIRE

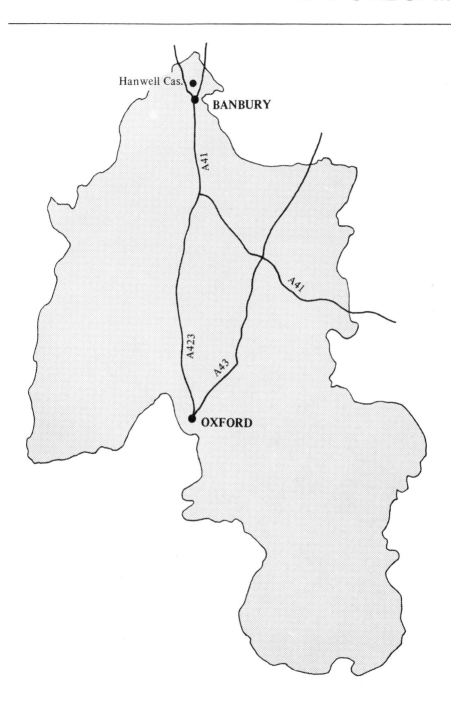

Hanwell Cas.

BANBURY

A41

A41

A423

A43

OXFORD

HANWELL

Hanwell Castle was built in 1498 for the Cope family and occupied by them until about 1820.

Unfortunately, only about one third of the Tudor house remains as a result of a severe fire toward the end of the eighteenth century when the destroyed sections were rebuilt in the Georgian style.

Used as a private residence, the castle is closed to the public.

RUTLAND

OAKHAM

Used as a courthouse for many years, the Great Hall of the old castle was given by the Lord of the Manor to the town.

The rest of the castle having long since gone, the chief point of interest of the Hall is the extraordinary collection of ornamental horseshoes adorning its interior walls. These date from the early seventeenth century until the present day and have all been given by Peers of the Realm in accordance with an old custom whereby every Peer passing through the town for the first time must leave a horseshoe, or the money to have one made.

SHROPSHIRE

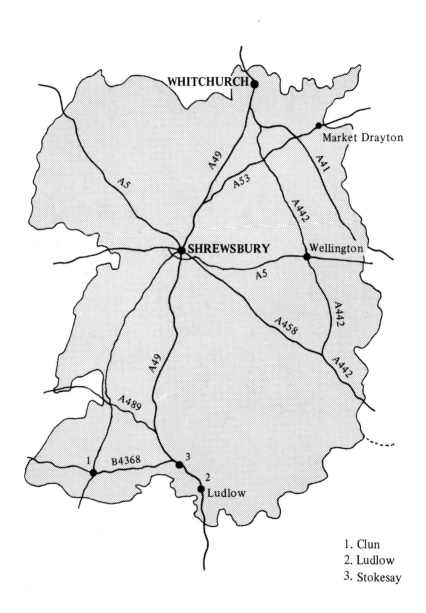

WHITCHURCH

Market Drayton

A49

A5

A53

A41

A442

SHREWSBURY

Wellington

A5

A458

A442

A49

A442

A489

1

B4368

3

2

Ludlow

1. Clun
2. Ludlow
3. Stokesay

The ruin of Clun Castle is skeletally stark in contrast to the great, undulating earthwork remains which surround it.

Dating from the thirteenth century, the ruined walls of two semicircular towers stand, forming, with the Norman Keep, an impressive picture above the river which once protected two sides of the castle from attack.

LUDLOW

Doubtless built as a consequence of the troubles around the Welsh borders, Ludlow Castle is a warm stoned, well preserved ruin attributed to Roger Montgomery, Earl of Shrewsbury and Arundel.

Scene of much minor squabbling throughout its early history, Ludlow passed, in 1425, to Richard, created Duke of York the following year. It was this Richard who, moving against the King, precipitated the Wars of the Roses, the decisive battle of which was nearly fought outside the walls of Ludlow. Had the two armies ranged against each other actually joined battle, the outcome of the war might well have

been decided earlier, if not differently. Richard's ally, Sir Andrew Trollope, however, opted to change sides the night before the battle was due to commence and the addition of such a veteran soldier and his supporters to the Lancastrian army caused the depleted Yorkist forces to suffer a severe defeat.

Although Richard was dead before the Wars of the Roses were over, his son, Edward, marched on London and seized the crown, later sending his son, Edward Prince of Wales, to Ludlow where he stayed for the next eleven years before being taken to London and murdered, with his brother, in the Tower.

Henry VII, by birth a Welshman and the first King of the Tudor line spent much time at Ludlow and it was to here that his son, Arthur, brought his bride, Catherine of Aragon.

The Civil War saw the castle besieged by the Parliamentary troops but, fortunately, it seems to have escaped the destruction which was visited on so many castles at this time, for we are told that, it was allowed to fall gradually into decay.

Clun

Ludlow

STOKESAY

Stokesay Castle is one of the oldest fortified houses (as opposed to castles proper) in England, the Great Hall dating from the late twelfth century, and it has what must surely be the most picturesque gatehouse in the country, particularly the timbered, late sixteenth century upper section.

SOMERSET

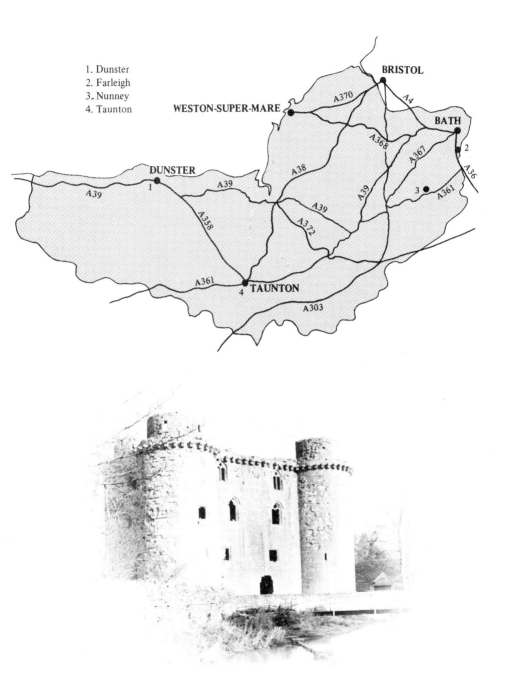

1. Dunster
2. Farleigh
3. Nunney
4. Taunton

BRISTOL

A370

A4

WESTON-SUPER-MARE

BATH

2

A368

A367

A36

DUNSTER

A38

A39

3

A361

1

A39

A39

A39

A358

A372

A361

TAUNTON

4

A303

Although there has been a castle at Dunster since about 1070, the present building dates very largely from the late sixteenth century when George Luttrell carried out an extensive programme of work on the site.

The Civil War nearly put an end to the castle. At the outbreak of the war, Thomas Luttrell held the castle against the King's forces until it seemed that the Royalist cause was going rather too well generally. Surrendering the castle, he changed sides and was later obliged to defend it against Parliament in a siege that lasted six months before the garrison were starved into surrender. An order was made for the castle's demolition some time later but this was rescinded after some of the battlements had been removed and, the following year, Luttrell was permitted to return to his castle after payment of a substantial fine.

Set in magnificent countryside, the castle contains many interesting and beautifully furnished rooms open to the public.

This must once have been a magnificent castle, large and strong and humming with activity.

Now it is a pair of ruined towers and a Gatehouse rising from lawns regularly trimmed and joined by foundations of walls long since pulled down.

Taunton Castle.

Nunney castle.

NUNNEY

This must be, without doubt, the most beautiful castle in the county and, although small, one which leaves a lasting impression of symmetrical sturdiness.

Atmospherically very much a part of the village, the castle stands surrounded by the still waters of its encircling moat close to a pretty stream. Its walls are honey coloured and mellowed by the passage of centuries. Its setting is ideal for visual effect but not for defence and its small size conveys a feeling of friendly strength rather than aggression.

TAUNTON

Taunton Castle, scene of one of Judge Jeffreys' famous trials during which, in two days, he condemned 508 out of 509 defendants to be hanged, drawn and quartered, now houses the Somerset County Museum.

Scene of many a battle, Taunton Castle has been subject to a number of alterations but traces of the old Norman Keep remain and the fifteenth century Gatehouse is the Museum entrance.

131

SUFFOLK

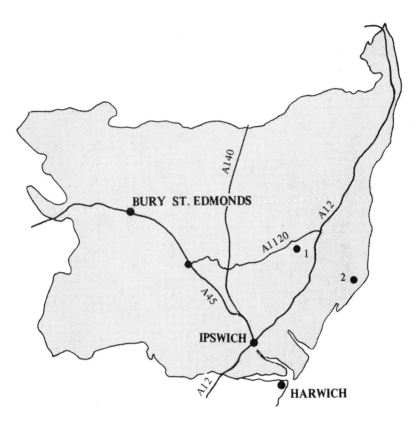

1. Framlingham
2. Orford

FRAMLINGHAM

Framlingham castle.

Here is another of those high-standing ruins which so delighted eighteenth century romantics and continues to attract crowds to this day.

Not over large, Framlingham was built originally in the early years of the twelfth century and rebuilt some two hundred years later. Apart from the massive Curtain Wall with its thirteen towers, there is little left of this castle, once occupied by the Howard family, Dukes of Norfolk.

ORFORD

The Keep is all that remains of Orford Castle, though it is just possible to pick out the original contours by the mounds and hollows in the surrounding earth.

Built as a bulwark against the Danes in the twelfth century, the castle served also to remind the powerful East Anglian Barons of the King's authority over them. The Keep, built to a unique, polygonal plan, has a massively impregnable air that could not have failed to impress mediaeval troublemakers and the Dungeon cum cesspit built into the thickness of a wall is unlikely to have gained a high reputation for the warmth of its hospitality.

Orford castle.

SURREY

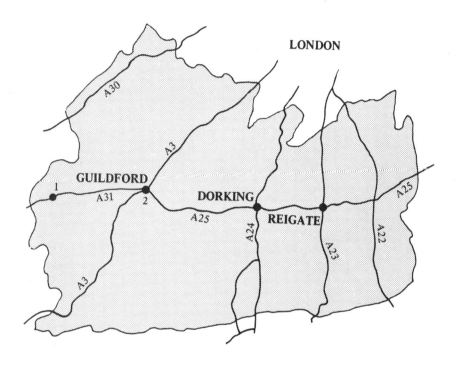

LONDON

A30

A3

GUILDFORD

A31

DORKING

A25

REIGATE

A24

A23

A22

A25

A3

1. Farnham
2. Guildford

FARNHAM

Built by Bishop Henry of Blois toward the middle of the twelfth century, Farnham Castle was intended to serve as a residence for himself and his successors.

The circular Shell Keep here is unusual in that its wall sheaths the usual Motte instead of standing on its summit — a device which would have allowed very little advantage to attackers managing to breach the wall.

Being a residence of the Bishops of Winchester, Farnham was relatively uninvolved with warlike activities, though it changed hands a couple of times during the Civil War before being slighted by Parliament.

GUILDFORD

Guildford Castle is one of those taken over by the local authority, surrounded by flower beds and benches and labelled 'a picturesque ruined castle . . . one of Guildford's many attractions.'

Dating from around the middle of the twelfth century, the rectangular Keep of Guildford has never withstood a single siege, though it was occupied for a time by the Dauphin when he came to England to dispossess King John.

During the early period of its life, Guildford was used extensively by the Kings and Queens of England, many children of the royal blood having spent considerable portions of their childhood here. Later it was used almost exclusively as a prison for criminals from Surrey and Sussex, suffering the usual dilapidations in the process.

Guildford castle.

135

SUSSEX

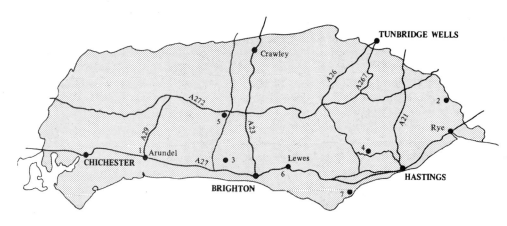

1. Arundel
2. Bodiam
3. Bramber
4. Herstmonceux
5. Knepp
6. Lewes
7. Pevensey

ARUNDEL

Arundel Castle, home of the Duke of Norfolk, stands in its great park above the traffic-shattered little town of Arundel.

Being continuously occupied through many centuries, the castle has benefitted from many additions to its structure beside having been kept in a generally good state of repair despite its having been several times besieged.

Pale, large and crisply kept, the castle dates from the eleventh century, when it was built by Earl Roger de Montgomery, another of the Conqueror's ubiquitous relatives. Early in the following century it was beleaguered for three months by the King, Henry I, and Robert — son and successor of Earl Roger — was exiled for rebellion. The squabble between Stephen and Matilda again saw Arundel besieged for a short time.

The third, and by far the worst, siege occurred during the Civil War when it was battered for almost a month by the Roundheads under Sir William Waller before the garrison was beaten and starved into surrender.

Extensively rebuilt by the fifteenth Duke between 1890 and 1903, the castle houses a beautiful library and a considerable collection of paintings and fine furniture.

BODIAM

Close by the River Rother, Bodiam Castle stands picturesquely in its lily grown moat which is large enough to be considered seriously as more of an artificial lake.

Dating from the end of the fourteenth century, the castle was built at the command of Richard II to protect the countryside from the possibility of French attack by ship up the River Rother, which was navigable as far as Bodiam Bridge.

The history of Bodiam Castle is remarkably sketchy; it would seem that its defences were only tried once during the Wars of the Roses — when its garrison apparently surrendered with little or no struggle — and again, during the Civil War when it was doubtless slighted like so many of its contemporaries.

Under the wing of the National Trust, Bodiam Castle is a most attractive spot to visit and no visitor should fail to spend some time in the small museum in the Caretaker's Cottage which contains, among other things, many relics of the excavations carried out here by Lord Curzon.

138

Bodiam castle.

BRAMBER

HERSTMONCEUX

A single, flint built monolith rises from the flat topped mound that was Bramber Castle.

Property of the National Trust, Bramber Castle overlooks the Vale of Sussex and, although almost nothing remains of the old masonry, it provides a pleasant and peaceful spot from which to admire the view; one of the finest in Sussex.

The guide book, obtainable from the nearby Potter's Museum, is worthy of note. Titled 'The History and Legend of Bramber Castle', it contains very little history and the legend is strongly reminiscent of the doomy plot of aVictorian novelette.

This crisp, brick built castle stands smartly and well maintained in pleasant grounds which alone are open to the public.

Occupied by the staff of the Royal Greenwich Observatory whose new, aluminium Isaac Newton Observatory provides a stark visual contrast to its walls, the fifteenth century castle was one in which the domestic amenities took a prominent place.

KNEPP

All that remains of Knepp Castle is a portion of a rectangular Keep on a large Motte.

It is unlikely that the castle ever achieved any great size, since its destruction was ordered as early as 1216 when the Lord, William de Braose, fell out with King John.

Herstmonceux castle

Knepp castle.

LEWES

The castle at Lewes is tucked away behind shops and houses which line the busy High Street, hidden from view and easily missed by the casual sightseer.

Built by William de Warenne, the castle is almost unique in having two artificial Mottes (Lincoln Castle also has two) and it formed part of the system of defence for the Sussex area in conjunction with Chichester, Arundel and Pevensey Castles.

There are virtually no remains of domestic buildings which were once standing within the castle walls but, thanks to the devoted efforts of the Sussex Archaeological Society and the Sussex Archaeological Trust, such fabric of the castle as remains is kept in a very reasonable state of repair for the enjoyment of visitors.

PEVENSEY

Pevensey Castle stands on the site of the old Roman Anderida.

Built soon after the Norman Conquest, the stone castle was the work of Robert de Mortain, a half brother of the Conqueror. Its walls withstood sieges by Simon de Montfort and Richard II but, as time wore on, the castle suffered sadly from neglect and the depredations of local builders in search of cheap, prepared stone.

The threat of the Spanish Armada caused a great flurry of activity at Pevensey and gun batteries were hastily installed here, one of the guns dating from that time still remaining.

The Second World War saw Pevensey Castle once again enlisted in the service of the country, masses of concrete being used to reinforce the ancient walls for use as 'pill boxes' against the likelihood of Nazi invasion.

STAFFORDSHIRE

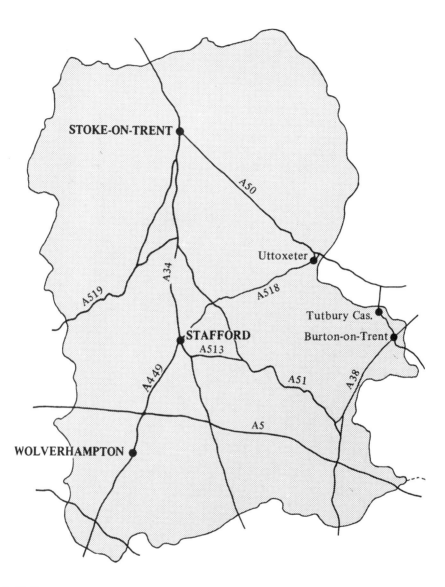

1. Tutbury

Some four miles northwest of Burton on Trent, on the A50, Tutbury Castle stands above the town, close to a charming little, eleventh century church.

A property of the Duchy of Lancaster, Tutbury Castle has a history dating back to the Norman Conquest, though the remaining fragments date mainly from the fourteenth and fifteenth centuries.

For many years a popular resort of Kings, Tutbury was owned at various times by John of Gaunt and Margaret of Anjou (Queen of Henry IV). Despite its having had a period of glorious history, the castle was in a sorry state of disrepair by the beginning of the sixteenth century, a Duchy surveyor submitting a report which was highly critical of the quality of repair work carried out in the past.

Mary Queen of Scots was imprisoned here for some time despite the protests of the Earl of Shrewsbury, who was Constable of the Castle, that this was no fit place to hold a Queen.

The Civil War saw Tutbury held for the King. When it was finally captured by the Parliamentarians, its demolition was ordered but, following the Restoration of the Monarchy. some repairs were carried out following which the castle has enjoyed somewhat desultory use until 1952, when it finally ceased to be used as a farm.

WARWICKSHIRE

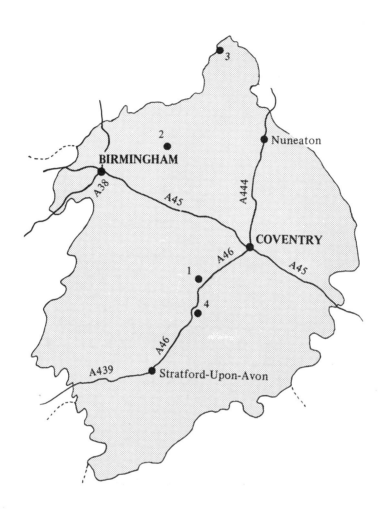

1. Kenilworth
2. Maxstoke
3. Tamworth
4. Warwick

This castle, in its days of greatness, was among the most important in the country and the list of those who were responsible for various building additions includes such as Simon de Montfort, John of Gaunt, Edmund Crouchback, Henry VIII and the Earl of Leicester, favourite of Queen Elizabeth I.

The first masonry building here was carried out in the second half of the twelfth century (1150 − 1175) and the castle was soon taken over as a royal stronghold to adjust the balance of power locally which was being siezed by the Earl of Warwick in his great castle some five miles away.

King John spent a vast sum (£2,000) on improving the defences and his successor, Henry III, gave the castle to his sister, Eleanor, and her husband, Simon de Montfort. It was at Kenilworth that de Montfort centred his military power during his battles with the King.

Following the death of the elder de Montfort, Kenilworth was besieged from spring almost until Christmas when, driven by starvation and dysentry, the garrison surrendered and the young Simon de Montfort fled abroad with his brothers.

Some indication of the strength of the castle at that time may be gathered from the fact that the full forces of both Church and State were employed in the attempt to batter it into submission. Beside the usual engines of war, barges were brought from Chester to launch a series of attacks from the 100 acre artificial mere which formed part of the defences and a great wooden tower was set up to permit two hundred bowmen to rain arrows at the defending garrison.

It was at Kenilworth that the unfortunate Edward II was imprisoned when he signed his abdication before being taken to Berkely to be barbarously murdered.

Elizabeth I visited Kenilworth several times to be entertained by Robert Dudley, Earl of Leicester and we are told that the entertainment laid on for one of these visits cost him £100,000. This was the period during which Kenilworth saw its greatest days. After Leicester's death, the fortunes of the castle declined steadily and, with the Civil War, the Parliament ordered its destruction. Although the order was never carried out fully, the castle was slighted and, despite a period of continued occupation, its fortunes declined steadily until, in 1958, Lord Kenilworth presented it to the people of Kenilworth. It is now under the custodianship of the Department of the Environment.

MAXSTOKE

Privately owned and maintained, Maxstoke Castle stands close to the golf course and about one mile south of the A47.

Licensed in 1346, the castle was built by William de Clinton, Earl of Huntingdon, and nicely illustrates the transition from the strictly military, concentric castles such as Harlech, which employed curtain walls, towers and massive gatehouses, to the Bolton or Bodiam type which incorporated domestic buildings within its square plan.

Here, inside the Curtain Wall, is a beautiful Tudor house in an excellent state of repair which contrasts nicely with the warm red stone of the Courtyard wall and old buildings.

The great Gatehouse at Maxstoke is still hung with the original oak doors on which can be seen traces of the metal cladding with which they were covered. The moss-grown Wall Walk is sound but slightly perilous and the recently-dredged moat contains fish to provide sport for a local angling group.

Very much a home, this small, delightful castle is not open to members of the general public.

Owned and used by the local Corporation as a Museum, Tamworth Castle was originally a Motte and Bailey fortification which developed over the centuries first into a fortified manor house and then into a country residence.

The Norman Shell Keep and Tower date from the twelfth century while other parts testify to the constant use to which the castle has been put through several centuries. The Great Hall dates from the reign of Henry VIII when it supplanted the area housing what are now known as the Royal Bedroom and State Dining Rooms as the castle's Banqueting Hall.

Twice in its history, the castle's destruction was ordered; the first time, by King John in his anger with the then owner, Sir Robert Marmion, for siding against him over the business of Magna Carta and, the second time, by Parliament after the Civil War, though there seem to be no indications that these orders were carried out.

Everywhere are additions and alterations in the styles of all periods up to the nineteenth century, including some fine seventeenth century carved work and a restored fifteenth century ceiling.

Warwick Castle, owned by Lord Brooke, son and heir of the Earl of Warwick, is a vast, magnificent structure which has been continuously developed since it supplanted the pre-Conquest timber fortification of Ethelfreda, daughter of Alfred the Great.

Possibly the most impressive single feature of the castle is Caesar's Tower, dating from the fourteenth century and rising one hundred and forty seven feet from the solid rock to dominate the other buildings and, indeed, the countryside around.

So great have been the influences of various Earls of Warwick on the history of England that any attempt to condense their story into a few lines would be doomed to failure. Suffice it to say that their great castle at Warwick stands as a fitting monument to their power and wealth and, stuffed with artistic goodies of all kinds of periods, it tends to have a numbing effect on the minds of visitors unaccustomed to such grandeur.

Warwick castle.

WESTMORLAND

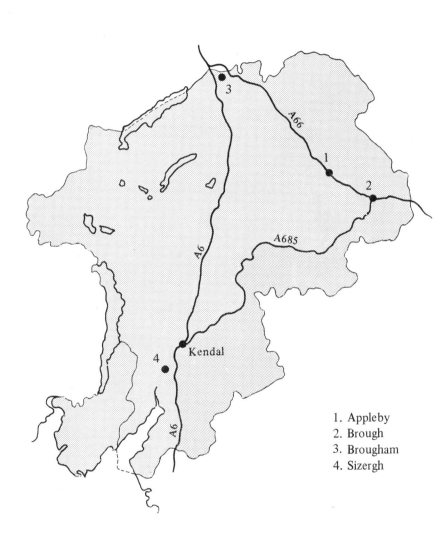

1. Appleby
2. Brough
3. Brougham
4. Sizergh

APPLEBY

Brough castle.

As a bulwark against the fierce and warlike Scots, Appleby town was built by Ranulf de Meschines in a sweeping loop of the River Eden, the castle being placed on high ground above the town. Later, during the twelfth century, the Norman Motte was altered to permit the building of a fine stone Keep and Curtain Wall with a Hall at the far end of the Bailey.

Twice, during the Scottish wars, the town was burned but there seems to be no record of damage to the castle itself during this period. The fifteenth century saw considerable work being carried out on the castle, but by the middle of the following century we find it described as ruinous.

A fine restoration house rose in the seventeenth century and further alterations and additions have in no way spoiled the imposing aspect of this impressive castle.

Appleby town is extremely popular with visitors, particularly during the month of June when it plays host to a vast gathering of gypsies who hold an annual Horse Fair in its streets.

152

Brougham castle.

BROUGH

This late eleventh century castle was a royal fortress of William Rufus. Destroyed by William the Lion in 1174, it was rebuilt and passed into the hands of the Cliffords, who also owned Appleby Castle.

The high Keep Gatehouse is empty but impressive and the curtains are well preserved for their age.

BROUGHAM

The ruin of Brougham Castle dates mainly from the late thirteenth and early fourteenth century.

Perhaps the chief feature of interest here is the unusual plan — there were outer and inner Gatehouses with a small Courtyard and then an Inner Court with a Tower. In about 1300, the Keep was pierced with large, Tudor style windows which must have seriously reduced its defensive qualities, and it is unusual to find the Gatehouses built so near to it.

SIZERGH

This fine Border Pele Tower is the property of the National Trust.

Dating from the late fourteenth or early fifteenth century, this is one of the largest and most impressive examples of defensive borderland building. It received additions during the Tudor and Elizabethan periods, however, which greatly increased its accommodation, enlarging it to enclose three sides of a square and, later, during the sixteenth century, further buildings were added to almost close the open fourth side.

The interior of the castle, beautifully furnished with a number of very fine pieces, contains some remarkably good Elizabethan woodwork.

Over page. Sizergh castle.

153

WILTSHIRE

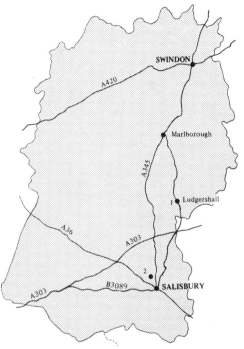

1. Ludgershall   2. Old Sarum

LUDGERSHALL

No more than a flinty crag dating from Norman times and traces of earthworks remain of this once important royal castle.

OLD SARUM

A mile or so to the north of Salisbury, Old Sarum shows traces of occupation since the iron age.

There is little masonry nowadays to remind the visitor of the importance of this site in mediaeval times, when it boasted a Cathedral and a royal fortress, but the carefully tended foundation courses reveal clearly the patterns of the various great buildings which were raised here from the eleventh century onward.

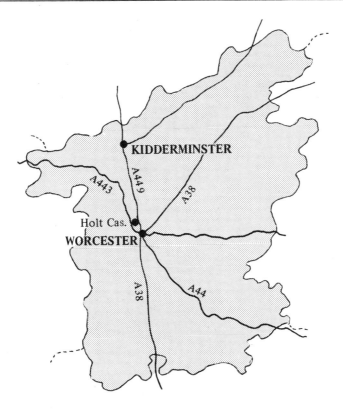

HOLT

Little is known of the history of Holt Castle, an unusually southerly example of a building of its type.

The chief feature of the castle is the fourteenth century Tower which stands forward of a later, fifteenth century, Hall.

YORKSHIRE

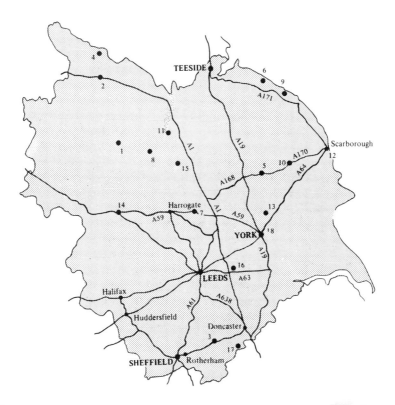

157

Raised by Richard le Scrope in the fourteenth century, this large castle is now part residence, part bar-restaurant and part ruin.

Standing amid high, wild countryside, the castle seems at first to be a warren of stairs, passages and chambers but these gradually order themselves into a carefully considered arrangement whose apparently random layout was designed purely to confuse unwelcome callers.

Much of the castle's interior is no more or less than an unused building — dusty, a bit crumbly but otherwise sound — while other parts are quite fascinating. Of particular interest to many visitors is the Wensleydale Kitchen, situated in the old Malthouse and Granary, which is a collection of nineteenth century furniture, kitchen implements and crockery put together by three local people as a hobby and open to public inspection.

Mary Queen of Scots was imprisoned at Bolton from July 15, 1568 until January 26 of the following year and, recognising the tourist value of this fact, nineteenth century restoration of the build-ings included the decision to designate a room — any room — as 'Mary's'. The second floor room of the Southwest Tower was chosen for this purpose and now houses a collection of local antiquities known as the Wensleydale Folk Museum. Since the State Apartments were situated not here but in the Northwest Tower, it is most probable that the unfortunate Queen never so much as set foot in the chamber that bears her name.

BOWES

Standing within the town of Bowes, the castle is visible from the main street and admission is free though there is a box for voluntary contributions just inside the gate.

A fairly minimal ruin of the Keep of a Royal Castle built by Henry II between 1170 and 1180, the building has had a circular stair replaced to the first floor level where a wooden walkway runs along one side.

Bowes castle.

CONISBURGH

A tall, pale Keep stands high above the ruined Curtain Wall of Conisburgh Castle; the whole structure standing on a high, steep mound which rises clear of the trees growing round its base.

The car park is situated a few hundred yards from the castle entrance, which is on the side of Castle Hill, furthest from the Doncaster—Rotherham road.

Built by William de Warenne (who was responsible also for Lewes Castle), the Keep here is unique, being circular with surrounding buttresses — probably to give the strength necessary for the inclusion of vaulted ceilings throughout in order to reduce the ever present risk of fire.

The entrance of the Keep is on the first floor, twenty feet above ground level and the higher floor levels are reached by means of a series of intra mural stairs each starting on the opposite side of the Tower to that on which the last ends.

Stone wash-hand basins are to be seen on two floors and the roof is equipped with a pigeon loft, an oven and two cisterns for water storage.

Virtually no other buildings remain

within the castle precincts but the massive size of the Keep is sufficient alone to ensure the popularity of this important castle.

Well signposted in the town, Helmsley Castle is a splendid ruin dating in parts from the early thirteenth century.

Mountainous earthworks provide a dauntingly impressive approach to the castle which, although slighted following its only siege in 1644, is still a large and magnificent structure.

The castle, beside the tall Keep, contains a well preserved, sixteenth century dwelling complete with floors which is kept plastered internally. It was doubtless here that the second Duke of Buckingham, the last owner descended from the castle's builder, died from a chill caught whilst hunting following his impoverished retirement.

Hidden away some half a mile from Kilton, the quite extensive ruins of a Norman castle stand in a wood.

The only condition of admission to the site is a signature in the visitors' book kept in the Gamekeeper's cottage close by at the entrance to the wood.

Greatly overgrown, little is known of the castle here, though some excavation work was carried out in the summer of 1972.

KNARESBOROUGH

The castle at Knaresborough dates from the fourteenth century, when it was rebuilt on the site of an earlier fortification.

Standing on a high bluff overlooking the River Nidd, the dominant feature is the massive Keep which stood, unusually, between two Baileys. There is an interesting theory that the Keep might have fulfilled an additional function as a Guardroom cum Gatehouse but the extensive alterations to the building, coupled with the damage which it has sustained, make accurate reconstruction difficult.

Like that at Pontefract, this castle is a possession of the Duchy of Lancaster, leased to the town in which it stands and used as an ornamental centrepiece for a spot of municipal horticulture.

MIDDLEHAM

Here is a small, quiet village dominated by a massive castle whose original shape and style has developed continuously over the years.

By tradition Edward, son of Richard, Duke of Gloucester (later Richard III), was born here in the round tower which is now known as the Prince's Tower and, later, died at Middleham.

The Keep is truly enormous – one of the largest in the country – and dates from the twelfth century when it was probably built by Robert Fitz-Ralph, grandson of the first Lord of Middleham Castle (there was an earlier fortification some five hundred yards to the southwest where traces of the earthwork are still to be seen). Unfortunately the Keep, like the rest of the castle, is extensively ruined but more than enough remains to convince the most casual visitor that this was once a stronghold of some of the most powerful men to have shaped British history.

162

Above and below Mulgrave.

PICKERING

Another of the really nice castle ruins, Pickering is à clearly defined example of the Norman Motte and Bailey type of fortification though, in this case, the Motte is positioned centrally between two Baileys.

The Curtain Walls and Towers date mostly from the twelfth and thirteenth centuries and the Inner Ward contains the remains of a twelfth century 'Old Hall'.

An interesting story is told by an eighteenth century topographer who reported that 'When it was besieged by the Parliament's forces, a large breach was made in the West side of it; and after it was taken, great quantities of papers and parchments, several of which had gilt letters on them, were scattered about the street called Castle Gate, and were picked up by the children who were attracted by the glittering leaves.'

MULGRAVE

Through the beautifully wooded estate of Lord Normanby, open to the public only on certain days, the old castle stands some three quarters of a mile to the southwest of the new.

Extensively ruined, overgrown with saplings, nettles, brambles and vicious six foot thistles, the castle has both Norman and thirteenth century features. Because of its overgrown state, this ruin is immensely exciting to those who like to feel that they are doing a bit of original detective work. Such danger spots as the well have been fenced off to reduce the risk of accident to a minimum.

This important and impressive castle was built originally by Robert de Romille, a Norman, but only one gateway is thought to have survived from that period.

The castle owes its present shape to an early fourteenth century rebuilding by Robert Clifford — an unfortunate man who was hung in chains outside the Keep at York to give it its name of Clifford's Tower. Owned and administered by Skipton Castle Ltd., the buildings and grounds are beautifully kept and maintained in an eminently suitable manner for the enjoyment of the public. To this end, an illustrated, step by step 'tour sheet' is available to direct visitors' attention to thirty-nine points of particular interest. Also available are copies of The Terms of Surrender and Delivery of Skipton Castle — a document setting out the agreement between the defending garrison and the Parliamentary forces when, after a three year siege, Sir John Mallory, the Castle Governor finally admitted defeat. Those with experience of modern warfare may well be surprised at the chivalrous terms granted to the losing side!

A mile and a half south southwest of Sherburn in Elmet, a mediaeval Gatehouse stands a short distance from the road and serves as the entrance to a farm.

Originally commanding the entrance to a mediaeval house, the building is decorated with attractive corbels but uninvited visitors may be excused the feeling that they are still unwelcome — signs prohibiting progress beyond the Gatehouse being prominently displayed.

SNAPE

Lying between the A1 and the A6108, about nine miles north of Ripon, Snape Castle is partly ruined and partly inhabited as a private residence.

The adjacent farmyard provides access to the Chapel, which is open to the public, and to the ruined sections of the castle buildings consisting of ruined towers at the northeast and northwest corners and a row of intercommunicating vaulted chambers.

Snape.

SPOFFORTH

A curiously pleasant castle, this, with some vaulted ceiling remaining and a single roofed turret. It was built in the late thirteenth or early fourteenth century and a licence to crenellate was granted to Henry Percy in 1308.

The village is attractive and quiet, the castle grounds neat and tidy. When the Custodian is not on duty, guidebooks may be obtained from an address indicated on a signboard by the castle entrance (always assuming that someone is at home).

Really a Fortified House, the remaining section of the building was originally just one side of a quadrangle. A curious feature is the way the building was constructed against a rock formation so that the entrance to the ground floor is down a flight of steps.

Richmond Castle, large and powerful, saw surprisingly little warlike action during its history — not even during the Wars of the Roses or the Civil War did it find itself embroiled in the clamour of war.

Built soon after the Conquest by Earl Alan, apparently to defend his men against the attacks of the English, the castle is important particularly in that it provides one of the most complete examples of early Norman masonry building in the country.

Apart from serving as the prison for King William the Lion of Scotland, the castle has virtually no political history, though its destruction was ordered by King John during the final year of his reign — an order which was never carried out.

SCARBOROUGH

Close by the remains of a Roman Signal Station, Scarborough Castle stands in a position of prominence in the town. Twice successfully besieged, the castle was taken by Parliamentary forces in 1643 and 1648.

The Keep, large and impressive, was built by Henry II between 1158 and 1175 as a position of strength from which the main entrance could be covered. The long wall which cuts across the headland is mostly Norman, but the half round towers probably date from about the thirteenth century.

Although the sea cliff on which the castle stands was originally thought to be defence enough and was left unwalled, it was noted in 1538 that there were three places where it could be scaled.

It was here that Piers Gaveston, a favoured friend of Edward II, was forced to surrender in 1312 and was then murdered under trust.

Richmond.

SHERIFF HUTTON

The ruins of Sherrif Hutton Castle stand, like four pieces from a gigantic, surrealist game of chess, above the houses of the village.

Part of a farmyard, the castle ruins encompass barns, with some of the vaulted castle chambers being used to house farm implements. Cellars, open to the sky, are used as rubbish tips.

Believed to date from about 1140, the first, and later replaced, castle was built by Sir Bertram de Bulmer and enlarged by Ralph de Neville, first Earl of Westmorland. Sheriff Hutton was used as a base many times by Edward III during his conflict with the Scots – a role to which its position was admirably suited, being close to the battle line but just far enough back to be a secure place.

Richard II stayed here often during his travels in the north and, after the battle of Flodden, the castle was granted for life to Thomas Howard, the victor, later Duke of Norfolk.

Falling into disuse after the conclusion of the wars with the Scots, the castle was dismantled for its valuable building stone and many of the houses around were built of materials taken from it.

167

Doubtless, the one-way traffic system through the streets of York were planned with considerable skill but a stranger to the town is likely to experience difficulty in finding himself outside Clifford's Tower unless he strikes lucky. For those with a poor record for finding needles in haystacks, I would recommend a route following the city wall – this may be indirect but it is, at least, reasonably certain of success.

Clifford's Tower, a quatrefoil Keep with a leaning, rectangular Gatehouse stands on a high Motte overlooking a car park and the Castle Museum. It was in an earlier, wooden tower upon this Motte that, in 1109, the Jews of York took refuge when pursued by a mob. Their security was short lived, for the citizens of York set fire to the tower's wooden walls and burned their quarry to death.

Ordericus Vitalis, an eleventh century chronicler, implies that the original earthwork here took only eleven days to be thrown up during a visit to the city by William the Conqueror in 1069. The same year, the Danes sailed up the Ouse, took both this and another, similar, Motte and Bailey fortification standing on the other side of the river and proceeded to sack the city – precisely the eventuality against which the castles were built.

TICKHILL

Behind a squarely impregnable looking Gatehouse stand the remains of what was once one of the most famous of all northern castles.

On earthworks probably established by Roger de Buishi, the castle dates from the twelfth century when it quickly became Crown property under Henry I and II.

Seized by Bad King John while Richard was away at the Crusades, the castle was besieged and taken by no less a personage than Hugh Pudsey, Bishop of Durham. The Civil Wars saw Tickhill once again embroiled in battle and, as usual, the castle was rendered unusable as a fortress by the order of Parliament.

A property of the Duchy of Lancaster, the castle is not normally open to the public.

York.

SCOTLAND

Examples of all the types of castles built in England and Wales in the early Middle Ages can be found in Scotland over roughly the same period and they were subject to the same changes both in siege tactics and defensive strategy until the middle of the fourteenth century. Clan feuds and the English Kings' determination to win control of the country, were part of Scottish history from the earliest days. That great castle builder, Edward I (and Edward III after him) campaigned in Scotland and such impressive piles as Bothwell and Kildrummy date from this time. Both the Concentric style and its evolution into the Quadrangular and Keep Gatehouse patterns can be clearly identified too.

From the late 12th century however, there was an introduction of small, fortified Halls, extremely simply designed and plain in appearance, which were the forerunners of the Scottish Tower Houses — buildings in a true and important National style, more significant in European terms than anything produced in England and Wales. That they are often called castles is perhaps misleading because, being small and only moderately fortified, they represent a family stronghold rather than a feudal fortress, which gives the lie to the reasons both for their emergence and their continued evolution long after serious castle building had ceased in England and Wales. The feeling that a specific problem has been solved, which communicated itself in such late English castles as Bodiam, Nunney or Kirby Muxloe, seems absent from the Tower Houses. Their plain, windowless fabric and simply fortified wall head represent a concept of defense so passive as to hardly permit any action at all. Yet it was adequate for a situation where fire was still the most frequently used weapon of attack and where a simply conceived entrance was sufficient to keep out all but the strongest intruder. A small Courtyard (or Barmkin) with a high wall accommodated simple buildings and cattle too, in times of unrest. The ground floor of the Tower consisted of storage space and very often its only apertures, apart from a trapdoor through the floor of the first storey, were air shafts situated within the wall to emerge on the outside at a comparatively inaccessible height. The main walls themselves are of necessity very thick, built both to take the thrust of a stone vault over the upper storeys and for security against the common forms of assault.

It is only when one enters the Tower that its marvels can be appreciated. An unwelcome intruder was confronted with all sorts of features to delay or bewilder him, for the narrow wheeling stairway, located within the thickness of the wall, might stop at one level, obliging him to cross the floor, before beginning again in the opposite corner. Their enemy's ignorance of the internal arrangements gave the defenders ample opportunity to harrass and surprise him from hidden chambers or galleries overlooking his route. Indeed the modern visitor will also be amazed, in some of the towers, at the great number of apartments large and small and at varying levels contained in what appears to be no more than a straightforward, Keep-like building from the outside.

The development of Towers continued in Scotland through the bloody years of the sixteenth century though a pause occurred after the Battle of Flodden in 1513 when many of the castle builders themselves were slain. However, as the influence of European, and particularly French, styles became felt through the French connections of the Stuart kings of Scotland, and as their owners sought more comfort at home, the decorations and domestic arrangements in Tower Houses became more elaborate and beautiful. Many buildings have survived in good condition and we are able to examine the variety of felicitous architectural details inside and out.

As hand guns became increasingly used, the necessity for strong fortifications at the Wall Head grew less and a defensive feature was often turned into a decorative one. Gables and turrets supported on bold corbels, little runs of crenellations and balustered galleries gave a Romantic appearance which was all the more impressive for its contrast with the plain superstructure of the building.

As more consideration was given to comfort and show inside, plans evolved with additions on one side or each end of the tower block, providing room for a spacious stairway and further chambers. Variations of 'L' or 'Z' shaped plans had the additional, practical result of providing flanking fire along greater stretches of wall but despite these developments (which took account of the dual needs of the owner) comfort eventually predominated and the Tower House in its final form, whilst standing as part of a strong tradition of military architecture, also represents the institution of a domestic style which was copied and, more often than not, debased, right into the first years of this century.

ABERDEEN

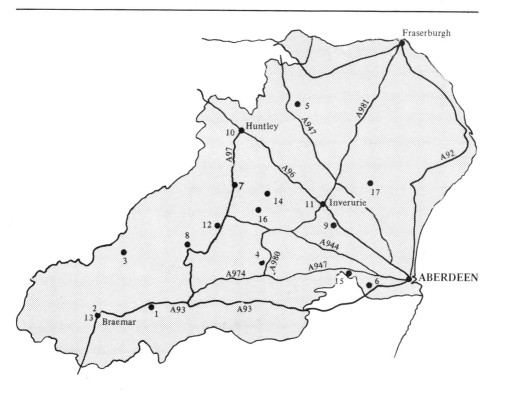

1. Balmoral
2. Braemar
3. Corgarf
4. Craigievar
5. Delgatie
6. Drum
7. Drumminor
8. Glenbuchat
9. Hallforest
10. Huntly
11. Inverurie
12. Kildrummy
13. Kindrochit
14. Leslie
15. Midmar
16. Terpersie
17. Tolquhon

171

Balmoral Castle.

BALMORAL, ABERDEEN

The Royal Castle of Balmoral, set in its picturesque estate on the banks of the Dee is only open at certain times, and offers the casual visitor a tour of the grounds only. The site of the original castle can be seen along with numerous memorials and rose gardens, individually attributed to past sovereigns.

BRAEMAR

Braemar.

Well into mountain country, Braemar is on the A93 about ten miles from Balmoral. The castle, visible from the road, has a long and interesting history, having been built in 1628 by the Earl of Mar, sacked and burned by the Black Colonel in 1689, and left for almost sixty years before leased to the Hanoverian Government for use as a garrison. The burned out interior of the castle was restored by John Adam, master mason and son of William Adam and brother of the famous Robert (of fireplace fame). Although leased to the Government for 99 years, the castle was returned to the family before this time was up and again established as a family home.

Having many common features with Crathes Castle, Craigievar was acquired by the National Trust in 1963 since when it has been open to the public.

It is a beautiful castle, beautifully preserved and furnished almost exactly as it was on the day on which the Trust took over. But, strangely, this detracts from the pleasure to be gained from seeing over it; there is the distinct feeling that one is prying into someone else's home and affairs. Everything is too recent and too personal, to be fully enjoyed without the slight feeling of guilt that even the most hardened ghoul must experience occasionally.

The derelict Tower House of Corgarf Castle, dates from the sixteenth or early seventeenth century and is encircled by a Curtain Wall with long narrow loopholes for musketry defence. It was of considerable strategic importance commanding the rivers Dee, Avon and Don, and boasts a long military history. In 1571, it saw the burning of Margaret Campbell and her family by Gordon raiders and in 1645 was the headquarters of Montrose. Corgarf subsequently nearly always maintained a garrison.

Craigievar.

Delgatie castle.

Drum castle,

DELGATIE

Open to the public only on Wednesday and Sunday afternoons from 2.30 to 5.00 p.m., this is a privately owned castle dating from the thirteenth century.

A mixture of warmly weathered red sandstone and white pebbledash, the castle has some nice features including the old dovecote front and sunseat.

DRUM

Another private residence, Drum Castle is one of the most impressive, and successfully built-on houses.

The Tower itself now stands as one side of a Courtyard. A large house joins the tower to form a second side, the Lodge and Gatehouse form the third and the fourth is bounded by a high wall.

Although the building is not over high, it has a massiveness which is quite impressive and the slightly overhanging parapet must have threatened any would-be attackers with the thought of the hurtful things which could be dropped upon their heads. The rounded corners, too had a practical defensive purpose.

DRUMMINOR

Drumminor Castle, fifteenth century stronghold of the Clan Forbes, is situated at Rhynie less than ten miles from Huntley, the headquarters of their greatest rivals, the Gordons.

The castle is nowadays open to the public at weekends, by appointment or 'when convenient' and, as a result of the superhuman efforts of two incredible ladies who spent ten years restoring the almost derelict building to its present excellent state, it is well worth visiting.

Bought in 1955 by the Honourable Margaret Forbes-Semphill, a fifteen generation descendant of the builder, the castle contains interesting collections of domestic appliances and kitchen equipment in the basement beside the period furniture, pewterware and small museum elsewhere in the building.

Sadly, Miss Forbes-Semphill was killed in a road accident in 1966, since which time the castle has been administered by her companion, Miss Wright of Inverkeithny, who shared the task of restoration.

Drumminor Castle,

Only about five miles from Kildrummy, where the Buchat joins the Don, stand the ruins of Glenbuchat Castle.

Another of the Gordon strongholds, this castle dates from 1590 when it was built by John Gordon who had inscribed on the staircase a latin verse which, translated, reads:

This house shows that I have every care of my health.
As wives cherish their spouses, I love life.
I declare death a stranger.
The godly love death and cry that love is vanity
But pain makes them weep forever.
Then live to love . . .
For love as lived, or beloved or believed,
Divinely shines.

The history of this castle echoes with tales of family strife, for in 1603, the laird, Adam Gordon, in an attempt to dispossess his mother of the castle, locked her up for thirty days and so terrified her that she feared to eat anything, believing her food to have been poisoned.

Twenty years later, Adam Gordon made another, successful attempt at taking the castle for himself when he managed to enter and throw out his younger brother 'in the act of telling some silver and gold' at his dining table. Despite the intervention of the Privy Council, Adam held the castle and estate.

A later laird, John Gordon, who was affectionately known as 'Old Glenbucket' distinguished himself in the Jacobite Risings and, after Culloden, was hunted through the Highlands with a price of £1,000 on his head. He eventually made his way to the exiled Jacobite court in France, via Norway and Sweden, where he died in 1750.

The castle was allowed to fall into disrepair during the nineteenth century but it is now owned by the Nation and under the care of the Department of the Environment.

Hallforest.

HALLFOREST

This massive, treegrown stump of a castle ruin stands in a cornfield just north of the B994 and about a mile from the junction of that road with the A96 as it travels from Aberdeen to Inverurie.

Granted in 1309 by Robert Bruce to Sir Robert Keith, Great Marischal of Scot-

land, the castle stood six floors high with walls seven feet thick.

HUNTLY

This vast, grand ruin was once the headquarters of the Clan Gordon and its inhabitants, the Earls and Marquises of Huntly, were among the most powerful landowners in the entire north. It is approached through an imposing arch in the centre of the town and stands in well tended grounds close to the gorge of the Deveron.

The Tower House section of the castle is strongly reminiscent of Drumminor, home of the rival Clan Forbes, with its large cellars and wide turnpike stairs and, preserved in the plaster of the cellar are scraps of graffiti which date back to the sixteenth century.

Stumps of long demolished walls provide good exercise for those interested in deciding what went where and the superb decorative stonework has been compared with that at Blois.

Huntly castle.

KILDRUMMY

Seat of the powerful Earls of Mar, Kildrummy Castle was once called 'the noblest of Scottish Castles' and, although dismantled after the first Jacobite rising of 1715, its ruin still has an imposing air of mellow majesty.

Although the height of the remaining walls is minimal, they are thick and permanent looking and rise behind a large cobbled area once a Courtyard

The Barbican with its deep draw-bridge pit will be of particular interest to students of mediaeval military architecture, as will the Chapel which projects at an angle through the curtain wall. The reason for this lies in the tradition that churches and chapels must be built on an east-west line and east-west was the way they were going to build this one regardless of the fact that the Curtain Wall of the castle ran at the wrong angle.

Edward I, that inveterate castle-builder, visited Kildrummy and saw the problem. He solved it by instructing the builders to erect a tower up against the projecting part of the chapel in order that it could not provide an enemy with a weak point through which to knock a hole, although the tower was never finished.

KINDROCHIT

The royal castle of Kindrochit at Braemar is an early authenticated example of a fortified manor. Robert II used it as a hunting lodge in the late fourteenth century. Later Sir Malcolm Drummond was permitted to erect a new tower house, the fifth largest in Scotland, within the framework of the older building, partly demolishing the old walls in order to do so. The plan of Robert II's castle is clearly visible as that of a great hall with square towers at all four corners.

Kildrummy castle,

LESLIE

About six miles off the A96, on the secondary road linking it with the A97 at Rhynie, Leslie Castle stands with some trees in a field.

Jackdaws wheel above and round the walls, swoop in and out through the empty window arches and perch, cawing, on every available place as though this were some great avian parliament.

A few traces remain of ornamental stonework, but it is the clustering of shapes and masses which makes this ruin attractive — this and the almost impossible balancing of some sections of the ruined walls.

Apart from this certain picturesque quality, Leslie Castle has little to recommend it to the casual visitor since it is a dangerous ruin of a fairly standard, L-plan Tower House.

Terpersie castle.

MIDMAR

    This Z-plan castle comes into view on the left of the A974 from Echt to Tarland.

    Unfortunately closed to visitors, except by special arrangement, the castle presents an extremely attractive picture, even from the road, of the fairytale quality of sixteenth century Scottish Castle building.

    Thought to have been built by George Bell, the castle may look romantic with its conical roofed, circular turrets jutting from the upper corners of the Square Tower and its crow stepped gables, but it should never be forgotten that a primary function of such features was to ensure that defenders could rain fire upon attackers without exposing themselves to danger.

TERPERSIE

    Terpersie Castle is situated behind some farm buildings along a narrow, un-likely looking road which serves only the farm.

    Greeny-gold lichens cover the walls, a tree grows through the space where once the great hall would have been, nettles reach from the interstices between the stones and farm paraphernalia leans against the crumbling sides of this never very large castle.

TOLQUHOUN

    Signposted from the A92, eight miles away, this castle, under the administration of the Department of the Environment, is situated approximately midway between Tarves and Pitmedden.

    The building has been unoccupied for only just over a century yet it has deteriorated considerably, despite having been placed in the hands of the then Commissioners of H.M. Works by the owner, the Marquess of Aberdeen, in 1929.

180

There is some confusion as to the date of the original building, but it is probably safe to assume that the 'Auld Tour' dates from the late fourteenth or early fifteenth century.

A plaque to the right of the Gate house proudly leaves no doubt as to the date of the later buildings:

'AL THIS WARKE.
EXCEP THE AVLD
TOVR. WAS BEGUN
BE WILLIAM FORBES
15 APRILE. 1584.
AND ENDIT BE HIM
20 OCTOBER. 1589.'

Much of the flooring remains in the various buildings, with enough stairs to allow a fairly comprehensive tour of the castle to be made and, on the way round, it becomes apparent that, although the castle is made to look rather ferocious with gun and pistol ports all over the place, it is really a domestic, rather than a military building. Indeed, many of the gun ports are situated in places where they can have had virtually no practical use at all and, on top of this, the restoration work being carried out under the direction of the Ministry of the Environment is contributing to the strange atmosphere of Toytown unreality already generated by this not unattractive castle.

Tolquhoun castle.

ANGUS

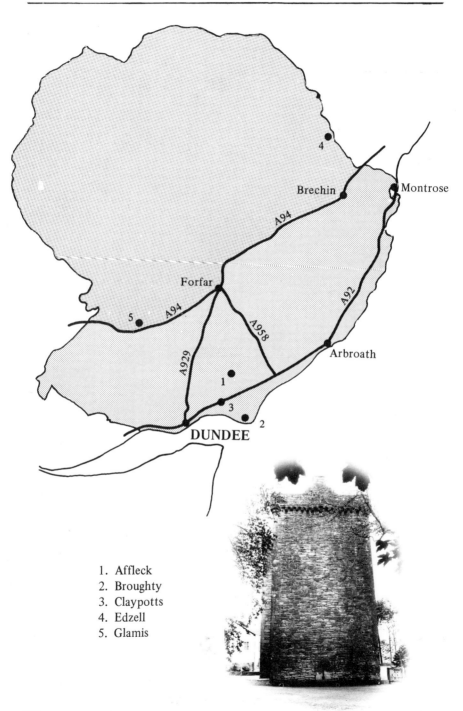

1. Affleck
2. Broughty
3. Claypotts
4. Edzell
5. Glamis

BROUGHTY

Situated in the least attractive part of Dundee, Broughty Castle is a rebuilt Tower House which, drab and grey, served as part of the defences of Dundee during World War II and now houses a small museum of disappointing content and primarily local interest.

CLAYPOTTS

This well preserved, Z plan Tower House was built by John Strachan and bears two dates: 1569 on the South Tower and 1588 on the North Tower which, considering the building was planned as a single unit, seems to suggest that it must have remained unfinished for a surprisingly long time.

Historically, Claypotts seems to have been involved in none of the troubles which were responsible for the damage sustained by other, similar, tower houses and this doubtless in some measure accounts for its good state of preservation.

Although empty, the watertight roof and sound walls have ensured the preservation of some interesting plasterwork within, in which can be seen marks suggesting how room partitions ran in the past.

Affleck castle.

AFFLECK

This small, late fifteenth century, beautifully preserved Tower House is privately owned and, unfortunately, no longer open to the public as a result of the careless and inconsiderate behaviour of some past visitors.

Claypotts.

183

Edzell castle

EDZELL

This beautiful ruin is a treasure house of heraldic and symbolic sculptures of the European Renaissance quite unique in Scotland.

The original building was the sixteenth century Tower House to which was later added a large Courtyard Mansion. Although the remains of these are interesting enough, it is the Pleasance which makes Edzell Castle the uniquely fascinating place it is .

Added to the earlier buildings by Sir David Lindsay, Lord Edzell, in 1604, the Pleasance with its Summer House, Bath House and incredible sculptured decorations must have contributed greatly to the financial downfall of the family who, in 1715, were forced to sell the estates, 'their affairs having fallen into hopeless embarrassment.' Sir David himself died in 1610 and even then he left his family in extraordinary debt', though he evidently made some attempts to alleviate the situation by granting rights to two German mining engineers to mine for copper, lead and alabaster in the glen.

Despite the depredations of the York Building Company, one time owners of the castle, and those of a garrison of Argyll Highlanders who occupied the building in the Hanoverian cause in 1746, during the second Jacobite Rising, many of the sculptured panels which decorate the Pleasance remain to give a delightful insight into the mind of a cultured Scottish gentleman of the early seventeenth century, illustrating, as they do, the planetary deities, the liberal arts and the cardinal virtues. There are also some fragments of fine heraldic carvings preserved against the north wall of the Pleasance.

Now in the capable care of the Department of the Environment, Edzell Castle and its attractive formal garden is beautifully maintained.

GLAMIS

The central, Tower house, section of Glamis castle is sixteenth century. The remainder has a little less credibility than the Loch Ness Monster. One has the distinct feeling that it has strayed from Disneyland.

Glamis castle.

ARGYLL

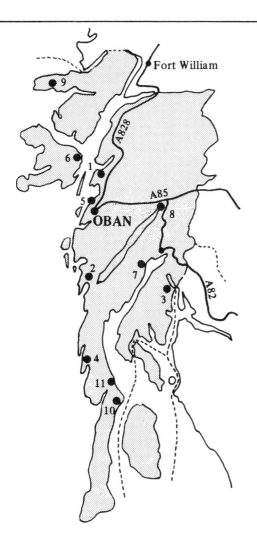

1. Barcaldine
2. Carnasserie
3. Carrick
4. Castle Sween
5. Dunstaffnage
6. Duart
7. Inveraray
8. Kilchurn & Loch Awe
9. Mingarry
10. Skipness
11. Tarbart

Barcaldine castle.

BARCALDINE

On a small peninsular in the Benderloch district of Argyll, Barcaldine Castle stands about a mile northwest of Ferlochan on the A828.

Privately owned, this small, domestic castle is used as a private residence and is not open to the public generally, although permission to visit may be obtained by writing. So small is it, in fact that it is surprising to find its presence indicated in a number of touring maps, particularly since it is of little interest either historically or architecturally.

CARRICK

Some eleven miles off the A815, through the impressively diabolical scenery of Hells Glen and then along an impossibly narrow road beside Loch Goil, Garrick Castle stands in what must once have been a truly magnificent and remote setting.

Now, alas, tin cans and waste paper spread outward from the surrounding caravan and camping sites and crudely written No Parking signs festoon the stone wall bordering the loch-side road, creating an air of gloom and despondency to which the castle itself seems to respond.

Carrick castle.

Castle Sween,

CASTLE SWEEN

Believed to be the oldest existing castle in Scotland, Castle Sween stands on an outcrop of lichen covered rock rising upon the east shore of Loch Sween.

Here, it seems, the wind always blows but this is no deterrent to the holiday-makers who rent the caravans drawn up like an invading army on the shoreward side of the castle. But invasion is no longer necessary, for the castle was largely destroyed by Sir Alexander Macdonald in 1647 and what remains is preserved and kept open to the public by the Department of the Environment.

DUART

The massive ruin of Duart Castle stands on a rock at the northeast angle of Mull and was for many years the principal stronghold of the Macleans.

Without doubt, one of the most powerful castles in the West of Scotland, it is possible that the Keep of Duart was built by Lauchlan M' Lean, founder of the house of Duart, who married Margaret, daughter of the First Lord of the Isles, in 1336, though it has been ascribed to an earlier, mid-thirteenth century builder.

DUNSTAFFNAGE

Dunstaffnage Castle stands on an attractive peninsula behind a Marine Research Laboratory and is set amid the carefully tended grounds which are a hallmark of Ministry custodianship.

A long, slow programme of restoration is under way and it is intended that the buildings should eventually house a museum — a worthwhile project, particularly in view of the castle's long and eventful history.

Traditionally the seat of the Dalriadic Kings after their arrival in Scotland from Northern Ireland in the sixth century, Dunstaffnage is said to have been the site where the Stone of Destiny was kept before its subsequent journeys to Forteviot,

to Scone and then Westminster. No trace now remains of the palace of these ancient kings, King Kenneth Macalpine, first king of Scotland, having transferred his capital to Forteviot in 850 AD after subduing the native Picts, and for the next three hundred years little is heard of Dunstaffnage. It is important to remember, of course, that the original 'castle' here was almost certainly a wooden affair, the existing stone castle dating from about 1290.

From 1110 onwards, however, Dunstaffnage was the scene of many a battle and many an intrigue between the Clan Campbell and the Clan MacDougall and then between the latter (who sided with the English during the 'Wars of Independence') and the Scottish kings. In 1320, following his defeat of the MacDougalls at a great battle in the Pass of Brander, Bruce laid siege to Dunstaffnage and, taking the castle, gave it to Alexander Campbell in whose family it remained thenceforth.

Close by the castle walls, half concealed by trees and shrubs stands a ruined Chapel and family Mausoleum. Although no firm date has been agreed by all authorities concerning the building of this structure it is widely held to date from the thirteenth century and, although most of the decoration has long since been eroded away, that which remains suggests that this must once have been an extremely beautiful building.

Although Dunstaffnage Castle is under the administrative control of the Department of the Environment, there are no guide books available from the castle itself and interested visitors would be advised to call at the Dunstaffnage Arms public house about a mile along the A85 towards Connel, where quite old guide books written in an enthusiastically historical style may be purchased for about five pence.

189

Inveraray castle.

Kilchurn castle.

INVERARAY

This very picturesque castle stands just outside Inveraray proper and is the focal point of a great many coach tours from all over the country.

KILCHURN AND LOCH AWE,

This twenty five mile long loch boasts a number of small islands, mainly at the north eastern end and, for obvious defensive reasons, three of the four castles to be seen in the area are situated some distance offshore.

The most important of these castles is that built in the fifteenth century by Sir Colin Campbell of Glenorchy. The island on which it stands rises from the marshy northern corner of the loch and, although the castle is not open to the public, it presents an attractive sight to travellers on the A85.

A mile or so to the southwest of Kilchurn stands another castle, truly ruined, this one, but again attractively situated upon a small, beautifully wooded island.

Mingarry castle,

Continuing southwest along the loch for a further twelve miles or so, Ardchonnel castle rises from its small island to almost meet the eye level of travellers on the B840. Situated only a short distance from the shore, this castle is built more in the tradition of the simple, quadrangular curtain with a corner tower and the years have added a respectable covering of ivy to soften its lines and make its appearance more inviting than it must once have been.

MINGARRY

On the southern shore of Ardnamurchan, between Ben Hiant and Beinn na Seilg, Mingary Castle stands, a ruined stump, across the bay from Mingary Pier.

Easiest approached from the sea, the castle has a landward entrance which is high up and would have been guarded by an overhanging timber bretache.

There are some very nice windows in the north wall, with some evidence of timber window frames.

SKIPNESS

Impressively situated in truly wild countryside, Skipness Castle looks out across Kilbrannan Sound toward the dark hills of Arran.

In a remarkable state of decayed preservation, the 13th century Hall House is used to house farm implements, and the nettle-grown Courtyard shelters horses from the wilder weather. Silence reigns supreme here, broken only by the sounds of wind and sea and the cries of birds as they wheel around the red sandstone walls whose edges and corners have been eroded by seven hundred years of frost, wind and rain into softly rounded shapes.

TARBERT

On a rise overlooking East Loch Tarbert stands an ivy covered stubbily ruined tower. Below, the fishing boats nudge the harbour wall in the finest picture postcard traditions and, across the loch, the craggy, heather-covered hills change colour as clouds cross the sun.

Skipness castle.
Tarbert castle.

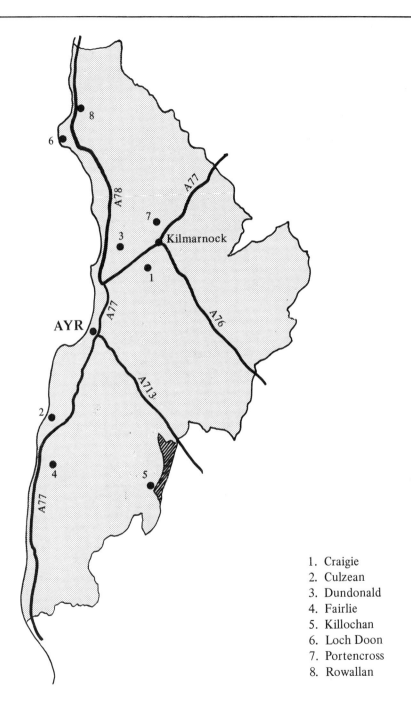

1. Craigie
2. Culzean
3. Dundonald
4. Fairlie
5. Killochan
6. Loch Doon
7. Portencross
8. Rowallan

Craigie castle.

CRAIGIE

This small ruin is situated in farm-
land between the A76 and the A77 a few
miles south of Kilmarnock.

The little that still stands is well
overgrown but the ruin has a friendliness
about it that is hard to ignore. The remaining stonework shows a high degree of
finish and there are indications of a fine,
Gothic arched ceiling, now gone.

Among the weeds is a barrel vaulted
cellar and, on the south eastern side, a
section of the curtain wall, thirty feet long,
fourteen wide and almost five feet thick,
lies in one piece, flat on the ground —
testimony to the strength of the mortar
used in these buildings.

As so often happens, the title Castle has been applied to Culzean more of a matter of courtesy than of fact.

The existing, Robert Adam, house stands on the site of an earlier tower house whose interior was described by Sir William Brereton, after a visit to the house in 1635, as having ' . . . no hall, only a dining room or hall, a fair room and almost as large as the whole pile, but very sluttishly kept, unswept, dishes, trenchers and wooden cups thrown up and down, and the room very nasty and unsavoury. Here we were not entertained with a cup of beer or ale . . . '

The present mansion is best described in the words of the Parish Minister, the Reverend Mr. Matthew Biggar, who wrote within a few years of the building's completion;

'This noble edifice is situated upon a rock, projecting a little into the sea, of about 100 feet in height from the surface of the water and almost perpendicular. The plan and design were given by the late Mr. Robert Adam; and such is the style of architecture, such the execution of the work, and the beauty of the stone, that it impresses the mind with delightful ideas of elegance, order and magnificence exceeding anything similar in the country . . .'

In 1945, the mansion was acquired by the National Trust for Scotland and, the following year, a top floor flat was prepared for the use of General Eisenhower for the duration of his lifetime as a token a Scotland's gratitude for the role he played as Supreme Commander of the Allied Forces during World War II.

Culzean castle.

Dundonald Castle.

DUNDONALD

Between the A77 and the A78, about ten miles north of Ayr, Dundonald castle stands upon a high, isolated hill around the bottom of which are clustered modern, boxy houses with rubber plants and wicker garden furniture.

The large, oblong Tower House was rebuilt in the fourteenth century by King Robert II (the first of the Stuart Kings), whose favourite residence it became, and it is notable particularly on account of the way the earlier, thirteenth century gatehouse was incorporated in the structure.

FAIRLIE

Kelburn castle, private residence of Rear Admiral the Earl of Glasgow, is situated on a hill to the east of the A78 as it leaves Fairlie.

Although it is not open to the public, the castle is visible from the excellent golf course which lies between it and the road and has the attractive, turretted appearance common to many of its type and period.

Kelburn Castle.

KILLOCHAN

Killochan Castle stands on the banks of the River Girvan about three miles from where the river enters the Firth of Clyde. The Lands of Killochan were owned for many years by the Cathcart family, at least as far back as the thirteenth or fourteenth century, as there was a charter granted by Edward Bruce about the year 1317 and confirmed by Robert the Bruce in 1324.

A condition of the latter charter was that the Baron should furnish the King "three sufficient spears on Christmas Day at our head Manor of Turnberry". Descendants of the Cathcart family lived at Killochan until 1954.

The main block, of sixteenth century origin, consists of five storeys, featuring two angle-turrets in the gables facing west and another to the north, each provided with shot holes. An unusual further feature of the structure is a circular tower to the south-east, crowned with a conical slated roof. Even more unusual is the fan-shaped window, only recently discovered, built into the 14 ft. thick west facing wall, complete with original iron Yett. Presumably, this would have been a means of obtaining extra light in the Great Hall of that period. The vaulted basement consists of old kitchen, cellars, guard room, armoury, and reputedly, a chapel. There are several minor turret stairs in addition to the main spiral staircase. Many secret panels and chambers have been discovered in recent years. A two storey wing was added during the eighteenth century to the north-west of the tower block. The whole has been carefully restored and is now in excellent repair.

LOCH DOON

Seven miles along a narrow road of the kind ominously termed 'other roads' by the makers of tourist maps, stands the small, eleven sided shell of a castle which dates from the fourteenth century.

Apart from its unusual shape, the castle's chief claim to fame is that it was moved and rebuilt, stone by stone, from its original position on a small islet in Loch Doon when the water level was raised by the great concrete dam at the northern end.

Situated as it is in the Southern Uplands, this castle makes an attractive spot for picnics and day trips, as the surrounding litter testifies.

PORTENCROSS

From West Kilbride across the A78, Portencross lies on the coast and looks toward Little Cumbrae Island.

The castle, a small tower, stands on a low outcrop of rock which juts out into the sea and is used now by fishermen as a store for lobster pots and other paraphernalia of their trade. The setting is extremely picturesque; a row of fishermen's cottages behind, blue-black water stretching away to the island, an old rusty cannon lying in the long grass and hordes of wheeling seagulls attracted by the incoming fishing boats.

An interesting feature of the Tower's interior is the way in which stairs were arranged to lead from the ground floor to the Battlements without interruption to the intervening rooms — an unusually civilised feature in castles of this age since one of the usually employed defensive features in castles of this type was a method of construction which demanded that anyone climbing to the top should be forced to pass through the rooms on the way up in order that unwelcome visitors could not pass unchallenged by the Master of the House.

The Castle on Loch Doon.   *Opposite: Portencross.*

ROWALLAN

A short distance to the north of Kilmarnock, Rowallan Castle represents the sixteenth and seventeenth century development of Scottish castles.

Small, attractive and friendly looking , the building appears more ornamental than aggressive and clearly was intended as a living, rather than a fighting, place (the forework, with its two chubby, round towers and rope decoration are particularly attractive) though the gun ports and sturdiness of the building indicate that defence was not ignored by the builders.

The castle stands in the beautiful Rowallan Estate and, although the public are welcome to view it from the outside, it is not yet open and 'Private' signs clearly indicate that casual visitors are not welcomed elsewhere on the estate.

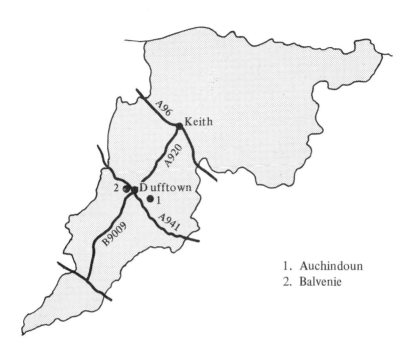

1. Auchindoun
2. Balvenie

Another well-signposted ruin, Balvenie Castle stands just to the north of Dufftown and close to a whiskey distillery which is also open to visitors.

More English in appearance than most Scottish castles, Balvenie was an ancient stronghold of the Comyns, though little beyond the Curtain Wall and great Ditch remains of their work, the present entrance dating from the sixteenth century.

Subsequent masters of Balvenie were the Black Douglases and the Earls of Atholl, who were Stewarts, and, in 1746, it was occupied by the Hanoverians for a time.

Although the old Curtain Wall is largely intact and the first floor levels remain in the old Gatehouse block, there are some dangerously unguarded drops and children should be discouraged from running on ahead of parents.

Below: The curtain wall which encloses Balvenie castle.

Auchindoun castle.

AUCHINDOUN, BANFF

The massive ruin of Auchindoun Castle is situated on the top of a conical hill which rises some 200 feet above the Glen of Fiddich, about three miles from Dufftown.

The castle has been roofless for nearly two hundred years and has become so dilapidated that restoration is considered impracticable. Although said to date from the eleventh century, the present remains are unlikely to be older than the fifteenth century. It was built on the L plan and was first owned by Ogilvy of Deskford before it came to the Gordons in 1535. In 1592, the castle was burned by the Macintoshes out of revenge for the murder of their chief, whose head is said to have been cut off and fixed upon the gate of Auchindoun Castle.

202

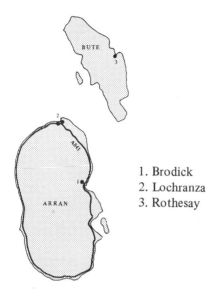

1. Brodick
2. Lochranza
3. Rothesay

BRODICK CASTLE

Brodick castle, a beautiful building splendidly maintained by the National Trust for Scotland, stands on the romantic Isle of Arran.

Prior to 1958, the Castle was the home of the Duke and Duchess of Montrose and it has been kept faithfully as it was — so much so that visitors tend to talk in hushed tones as though they expect to be asked the reason for their invasion at any moment.

Brodick Castle stands on a site which was once a Viking stronghold before being yielded to the First Lord of the Isles. Robert Bruce stayed here to rally support after his defeat at Methven in 1306 and the castle was twice sacked by the English.

Rothesay Castle

ROTHESAY

In its earliest days (prior to the year 1300), Rothesay Castle received a certain amount of attention from the Norsemen who are recorded as having captured and lost it at least twice. Later, the Scots and the English each took possession on various occasions, each adding bits to the building as they saw fit until, in 1512, James IV of Scotland ordered work to begin on the last major addition, the great tower known as 'le dungeon'.

By this time, the castle had been placed in the hands of the noble family of Bute and the office of Hereditary Keeper of the Castle is still vested in the Marquis of Bute, though the building is nowadays in the guardianship of the Department of the Environment.

Visitors from the mainland will find the castle (the only extant example of a surviving Shell Keep in Scotland) only a

short distance from Rothesay Pier and it is the Great Tower of James IV's creation which, alone bigger than many of the more typically Scottish castles forms the Gate-house and dominates the remainder of the structure. Most of the buildings contained in the Courtyard are now little more than lines of foundations, but the Chapel still stands and the northwest tower has been well preserved.

Perhaps the most impressive single feature of Rothesay Castle however, is the reconstructed first floor of the Great Tower

The plastered walls and regal pro-portions of this vast hall have the effect of making the sixteenth century seem sud-denly alive and real, providing a strong argument in favour of a certain amount of sincerely undertaken and accurately carried out restoration on buildings of this kind.

CLACKMANNAN

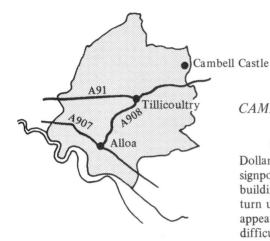

● Cambell Castle

A91

A907 A908 Tillicoultry

Alloa

CAMPBELL CASTLE

Up a steep, uneven road rising out of Dollar (at the time of writing, confusingly signposted owing to the demolition of a building on which the sign indicating a left turn used to be), Campbell Castle suddenly appears through the trees and makes the difficulty of finding it all worthwhile.

Cars must be left at the top of a neighbouring hill and visitors have a fair, steep walk to the castle which is in a good state of repair.

DUMBARTON

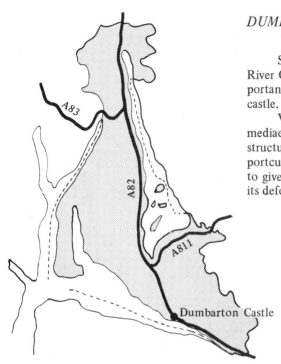

DUMBARTON

Standing on its basalt rock in the River Clyde, Dumbarton Castle was an important stronghold and mediaeval royal castle.

Virtually nothing remains of the mediaeval buildings, the oldest surviving structure being the fourteenth century portcullis arch, and few records survive to give a clear idea of the early fortress or its defensive systems.

Dumbarton castle from the N.W., drawn by John Slezer, 1693.

DUMFRIES

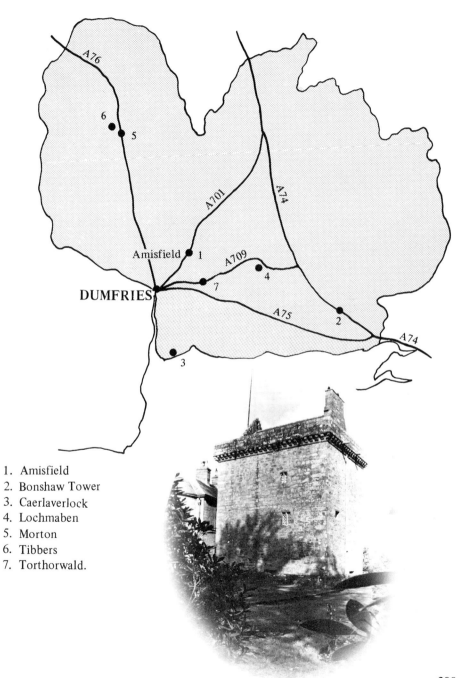

1. Amisfield
2. Bonshaw Tower
3. Caerlaverlock
4. Lochmaben
5. Morton
6. Tibbers
7. Torthorwald.

Bonshaw Tower

AMISFIELD

Amisfield

This four storeyed, rectangular Tower House indicates the direction taken by Scottish builders as the demand for home comforts overtook that for impregnable defence.

Although in 1600 (when this tower was erected), walls were still built to a great thickness and the defensive advantages of height were not overlooked, windows can be seen to be somewhat larger than hitherto and, inside, there are more rooms in which greater emphasis is placed on convenience and comfort for the inhabitants. The four circular turrets adorning the corners of the building owe their existence partly to the wish for additional rooms (dressing rooms and so on) and partly to the ingrained habit of defence since they offered a splendid vantage point from which to fire upon attackers anywhere round the walls of the building.

Part of a private residence, Bonshaw Tower is situated a short distance off the A74 up a small, tree-lined road marked 'Kirtlebridge'.

Following the road for a short distance, beneath some high stone arches and past a nice church, the tower appears quite suddenly above the hedges to the left, and its excellent condition is due in part to the fact that it adjoins the house and has remained in the possession of the Irving family for a great many years.

Although quite small in size when compared with such as Craigievar, this is a splendidly stout little building which was restored in 1896 by John Beaufin and Agnes Irving who resisted the temptation to convert defensive arrow slits into windows, leaving the exterior of the building in a state very near to the original.

Caerlaverock Castle, under the protection of the Department of the Environment, stands surrounded by a reeded moat amid billiard table lawns above the Blackshaw Bank in the Solway Firth.

Besieged by Edward I in 1300, the castle is considered to be one of the best examples of mediaeval secular architecture in Scotland and, although now largely ruined, has a beautiful Inner Court overlooked by some of the finest early classical renaissance work to be found in the country, which was added in the seventeenth century.

Electric lighting has been installed in some of the gloomier areas and, owing to the low wattage of the bulbs used, this serves strangely to exaggerate the massive darkness of Guardrooms and Donjon.

Caerlaverock castle.

Caerlaverock

LOCHMABEN, CASTLE LOCH,

Not far from Ecclefechan, birthplace of Thomas Carlyle, is the small, triangular Lochmaben, Castle Loch, and, heading South along the 7020, a turning sign-posted 'Castlemains' leads to the attractive ruins of this loch-side castle probably built by Edward I as part of his Scottish operation early in the fourteenth century.

Little remains now of this small fortress apart from some sections of ivy grown wall and two rather massive arches spanning one of the four ditches which at one time carried the waters of the loch round the castle as a defensive measure. Between these arches was the Drawbridge which would have been counterpoised, the weighted end lowering into the still-visible pit below them.

This is one of those castles which provides a wonderful focal point for a picnic excursion. Plenty of trees and nettle-free grass abound and permits for fishing may be obtained at the Castle Garage, situated at the northern end of the loch.

About fifteen miles out of Dumfries the A76 passes through Carronbridge, a minimal hamlet, just beyond which it is joined by the A702. About a mile or so on this road is the crossroads at Holestane and from here most maps become rather vague. Intrepid investigators, however, will pursue the road which appears to peter out and, when it does in fact do so, will follow the track leading uphill through young fir trees and heather until they see, across a field on the left, the walls of Morton Castle.

This is without doubt one of the most pleasantly sited of all the Scottish inland castles and, although the great Gate house has gone, and little remains but a high quadrangle of walls, it is one of those castles which sticks in the mind for some reason not fully known.

Historians and students of mediaeval architecture are unlikely to find much here to satisfy them but romantics and dreamers in search of a setting for their quiet fantasies are certain to enjoy this rarely visited, tree-grown ruin.

It is difficult to believe that the mound of rubble at Tibbers was once a stout Gatehouse Castle, built by Sir Richard Siward in 1298 and an important link in the chain of English fortresses established to control the wild Scots in the south western corner of their country.

The ruins remain, grass grown and derelict in a wood, a playground for local children, who, with splendid contempt for historical accuracy, blaze away at each other with plastic machine guns from behind the stumpy walls and fallen towers.

TORTHORWALD

Among the many ruins of fortified towers with which Scotland abounds, that at Torthorwald is a fairly typical example and it can be seen from the A709 about five miles northeast of Dumfries. Roofless and with two walls largely fallen away, the structure is in a rather unsafe condition and great care should be exercised by any tempted to leave the car for a closer look.

In its original state (it was built in 1340), the tower would have relied for its defence primarily on the system of surrounding ditches and ramparts which are now barely traceable in the field in which it stands.

Torthorwald.

EAST LOTHIAN

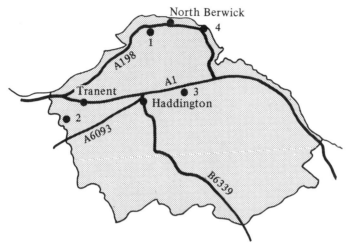

North Berwick

1. Dirleton
2. Elphinson
3. Hailes
4. Tantallon

Dirleton castle,

DIRLETON

The close cluster of powerful Towers with their appended buildings at Dirleton represent some four hundred years of living and building by three wealthy and powerful families; the de Vaux, the Halyburtons and the Ruthvens.

Built of stone from an early date by the de Vaux family, Dirleton was one of the most formidable Scottish castles of its time and one which was thought to be proof against the stone throwing siege engines of the thirteenth century. In spite of this, however, Bishop Anthony de Beck of Durham laid siege to the castle and, in 1298, took it for Edward I of England.

Garrisoned for England until 1311, the castle fell to the army of Robert the Bruce who probably destroyed parts of the fabric in accordance with their usual policy of rendering such buildings useless to their English enemies.

John Halyburton married the heiress of Dirleton and was killed at the Battle of Nisbett in 1355, his son, also John, obtaining in 1382 a protection for the castle and the Barony of Dirleton from King Richard II of England. Throughout the fourteenth and fifteenth centuries, members of this family were responsible for extending the castle's buildings to include the Vaults, Great Hall and the remodelled entrance.

In 1515, one third of the Barony of Dirleton, and its castle, passed to the Ruthven family who also added their quota to the building. The Ruthvens were involved in a number of political plots and wrangles including the murder of Queen Mary's favourite, Riccio, in 1566; The Raid of Ruthven, in which an attempt was made to remove the young King James IV from the influence of the Earl of Arran; the attempted seizure of Stirling Castle which resulted in the Earl's execution in 1585 and the Gowrie Conspiracy of 1600 which caused the two eldest sons of the family to lose their lives in an alleged attempt on the King's life.

In 1649, a number of people imprisoned at Dirleton, having been charged with witchcraft, were unfortunate enough to be brought to the attention of a Witchfinder named John Kincaid. Finding the Devil's Mark on each of the accused, Kincaid persuaded them to confess after which they were strangled and burned at the stake.

Dirleton housed a band of Royalist 'Moss Troopers' during the Civil War who made a practice of harrying Cromwell's army. On November 9, 1650, Major General Lambert set up a battery of great guns and, the following morning, the Castle fell.

ELPHINSTONE

If the name of this castle sounds as though it comes from the Lord of the Rings, the cunning arrangement of its interior must only serve to heighten the impression.

There are small rooms set into the walls of the building and intriguing spy holes and 'luggies' dotted here and there — the flue of the fireplace in the Great Hall, for example, conceals a small chamber with a window from which the Hall may be overlooked, and there is a spy hole which opens off the wheel stair adjoining the fireplace.

Luggies, as their name implies, are small listening holes in walls.

By reason of the arrangement of the stairs, intruders would be at a grave disadvantage in this castle for, in order to make the journey from lower to upper floors, they would have to climb a section of interrupted stair, cross each intermediate floor to reach the next section of the stairs and negotiate doors and defended passages at every level.

HAILES, EAST LOTHIAN

Hailes Castle, on the bank of the River Tyne, follows a rectangular plan; consisting of a stout Curtain Wall and a bold square Keep.

Hailes castle.

Tantallon castle.

TANTALLON

Situated atop a one hundred foot high promontory, Tantallon Castle was protected on three sides by the sea.

Dating from the fourteenth century, the ruin is fairly minimal now, little remaining beyond the great Gatehouse and its flanking Curtain Walls, possibly built by William, the first Earl of Douglas, who may well have been influenced in his choice of design by the great French chateaux of similar date.

Little important action seems to have taken place at Tantallon until 1491, when the castle was besieged by King James IV, though the outcome of the siege appears to be uncertain, for in 1492, Archibald, Fifth Earl of Angus (the besieged party) was made Chancellor of Scotland.

In 1528, Tantallon was again besieged by the forces of the Crown for twenty days but to no avail. Having failed in their purpose, the attacking army packed up to go home when Angus called one hundred and sixty of his followers from the castle and captured the artillery train as it departed. The following year, Angus surrendered the castle to the King and, for the following fourteen years, the castle was retained by the Crown.

Several times the castle changed hands after this until, in 1651, its walls were severely battered by Cromwell's artillery after which it was allowed to fall into ruins.

FIFE

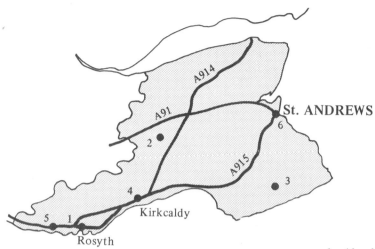

St. ANDREWS

A914

A91

A915

Kirkcaldy

Rosyth

2

4

5 1

3

6

1. Aberdour
2. Falkland
3. Kellie
4. Ravenscraig
5. Rosyth
6. St. Andrews

ABERDOUR

The oldest part of this attractive Scottish castle is the ruined fourteenth century Tower House to which, in succeeding centuries, the other parts of the building were added. Less than a century after its final completion, the castle was burned and abandoned in favour of nearby Aberdour House.

The guide book produced by the Department of the Environment contains some interesting details of the castle's history, including a fascinating Builder's Estimate prepared for the Earl of Morton in 1690.

Above: Aberdour castle.

FALKLAND, FIFE

The Palace of Falkland stands in the outskirts of a small, picturesque, cobbled stone village. The foundations of an early castle still remain, exposed as the result of excavation carried out over thirty years ago. The tower is early thirteenth century being twice built during that period when it was once levelled to the ground by English invaders. Other foundations include the base of a circular Well Tower to the east connected by a Curtain Wall to a second circular tower to the north.

Falkland was much extended during the second half of the 15th century when the great Quadrangle and Gatehouse were built. The old castle was gradually abandoned and the new castle became a royal residence until 1603. Since then it became partly ruinous, until restoration work during the nineteenth century brought it up to its present state.

Kellie castle.
Falkland Palace.

KELLIE, FIFE

Two miles north of St. Monans, Kellie Castle faces southward across the estury of the Forth. For a long period the castle was the Fifeshire seat of the Lords Oliphant followed by the Erskines, Earls of Kellie. The castle was abandoned after 1829 when the seat of the Earl moved to Allon. The castle was allowed to decay for 49 years until it was leased by the late professor Lorimer of Edinburgh University who undertook its restoration. The oldest portion of the castle is the North Tower which may be as early as 1360 though many argue that it dates from the sixteenth century. The Southwest Tower and other extensions along the course of the wall were added in 1573 by the fifth Lord Oliphant.

On a rocky promontory jutting into Kirkcaldy Bay stands Ravenscraig Castle. The sides rise a sheer 80 feet above the beach on two sides, the third falling off in a series of steep terraces, and a wide ditch protects it on the landward side.

Huge round towers, their walls nearly 14 feet thick, flank the castle at each end joined by a central building. The Donjon Tower, on the west side, was where James II's queen, Mary of Guildres, spent her widowed years.

The castle was protected on the landward side by a high parapet wall with wide-mouthed gun embrasures. To seaward there was less danger of attack and there is little evidence of any defensive preparations.

After Mary's death in December 1463 the castle was acquired by King James III who gave it to William, Earl of Caithness and Lord St. Clair in recompense for Kirkwall castle and the Earldom of Orkney.

Ravenscraig castle.

Rosyth castle

ROSYTH CASTLE

Built on a small, rocky island, Rosyth Castle has since found itself established firmly on the mainland owing to a land reclamation scheme in connection with the Admiralty Dockyard.

The chief remaining building is the Old Tower which stands sharp and square in the northeast corner of the Courtyard and which is entered now by means of a small door on ground level, though this originally gave access only to the storeroom on the ground floor. This tower, dating from the fifteenth century is the oldest part of the castle and doubtless, with its long since gone Barmkin, formed the residence of Sir David Stewart who was confirmed in his Barony of Rosyth in 1428.

There is a fine, square dovecote, dating from the sixteenth century, close to the castle walls, with barrel vaulted roof which is covered with flagstones.

Rudera Arcis Sancti *ANDREÆ.*   The Ruins of the Castle of S.t *ANDREWS.*

St. Andrews castle

ST. ANDREWS

The rocky-looking, ruined castle of St. Andrews dates chiefly from the sixteenth century, though the site was developed more or less continuously from the thir - teenth century when the first castle was built by Bishop Roger as a residence for himself and his successors.

During the Wars of Independence, the castle was captured, recaptured, dismantled and rebuilt by both English and Scots until, after Bannockburn, it was occupied and restored by Bishop William Lamberton, a Scottish patriot of some distinction.

Again falling into English hands, it was rebuilt in 1336 but, the following year, the castle was destroyed by the Scots as part of their scorched earth policy.

For some fifty years, the castle re-mained in a ruinous state to be rebuilt by Bishop Walter Traill. James I and James II both spent some time at St. Andrews, which also served as a prison during its lifetime,

besides being the scene of some of the most lavish living seen in Scotland. The famous 'Bottle Dungeon', so called for the way it widens toward the bottom, extended its rather dubious hospitality to a number of religious and political prisoners including George Wishart, who was burnt outside the castle walls, and John Roger, a Black Friar who was murdered secretly in its depths.

Another feature of great interest at St. Andrews is the mine and counter mine tunnelled through the rock beneath during a siege of 1546 — 1547. Discovering that the attacking forces were driving a tunnel with the intention of breaching the castle fortifications in several places, the defend-ers drove a number of shafts of their own until they succeeded in breaking through to the attackers' tunnel. Visitors may enter the resulting galleries which are lit by electricity and considered perfectly safe.

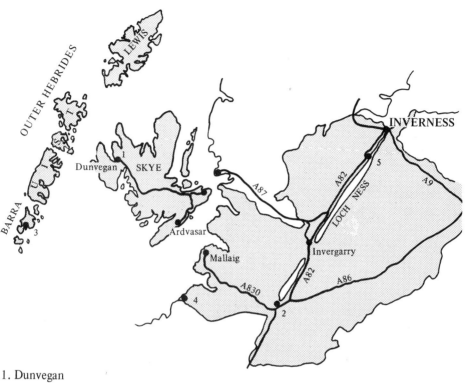

1. Dunvegan
2. Inverlochy
3. Kisimul
4. Tioran
5. Urquhart

Dunvegan castle

DUNVEGAN

Dunvegan Castle, on the Isle of Skye, has been the home of the Chiefs of Mcleod for over 700 years, though the name Dunvegan is thought to refer to an earlier time when the Vikings held sway over the Hebrides.

Naturally, any building inhabited for that length of time will have undergone numerous changes and Dunvegan is no exception. Although it is still a magnificent building, much work was undertaken during the eighteenth and nineteenth centuries which has detracted somewhat from the mediaeval appearance of the castle as it must have been prior to that time.

How much nicer is the atmosphere of this fine castle than that of many others which (with the best will in the world) have been preserved by bodies other than owner occupiers. Here we see a truly living building rather than a museum exhibit and it is only to be hoped that, with the fresh impetus given to the Clan spirit in recent years, this grand old building will continue to see active service for many more centuries.

Inverlochy castle.

INVERLOCHY

Scene of Montrose's victory over the Campbells on February 2, 1645, Inverlochy Castle stands just off the A82 about two miles northeast of Fort William.

Smelling like a sewer and thickly littered with a wide variety of twentieth century rubbish, the castle is not officially open to the public. Unfortunately it is not closed to the public either and, in consequence, it has become, without exception, the most unsavoury historic site in the British Isles.

226

KISIMUL

Seeing to rise right out of the sea, Kisimul Castle perches on a small rocky offshore island in Castlebay, Barra. The castle walls, which rise sheer to their Battlements, follow the contour of the rock on which it stands.

The Keep stands on the south side, being half within and outside of the Curtain Wall. On the opposite side of the castle, two small round towers project from the Curtain, and the Gateway, though now blocked, was sited next to the Keep.

Although there are no accounts of its building, it is known to have existed from the early part of the fifteenth century. The machicolations above the entrance Gateway and above the doorway into the Keep, and the Courtyard buildings, were all added later, in the seventeenth and eighteenth centuries.

Extensive restoration work is now being carried out by the present owners Mr. Robert L. MacNeil, the MacNeil of Barra.

Tioran castle.

TIORAN

A long drive through some of the most stagily wild countryside in Britain (west from Fort William to Lochailort and then along the coast on the A861, following it round to Blain before branching off right to head for the waters of Loch Moidart), and Tioran Castle comes into view on an outcrop of rock which juts from the sand at low tide to be cut off by shallow water as the sea rises.

This is a truly impressive setting for a castle and the partly restored walls of Tioran do fair justice to it. Unfortunately, the castle appears to be untended, the restoration dating from the latter end of the last century, and its exposed position is likely to cause steadily more serious deterioration as the years pass.

Interesting features are the massive Keep, vaulted Basement and the holes along the upper reaches of the parapet which would have served both as drainage for the wall walk and housings for the timbers of a hoarding to be used in times of attack.

URQUHART

Urquhart Castle stands on the end of a peninsula jutting into Loch Ness; a site which has revealed traces of Iron Age habitation.

This really is a remarkably attractive ruin, commanding a view almost from Inverness to Fort Augustus. It was this factor which, combined with the tactical advantages of the site, caused Urquhart Castle to play a prominent part in the history of Scotland.

During the Wars of Independence, the castle changed hands several times, sustaining damage and being repaired each time until, during the second Wars of Independence, it was one of the few castles to be successfully held against the English for the duration. In 1346, the Barony reverted to the Crown and, during the following hundred years, sums of money are recorded as having been spent on repairs and additions to the castle.

The conflicts between the Scottish Crown and the Lords of the Isles caused Urquhart Castle to become once again the scene of bloody battles during which much of the Great Glen was laid waste and its inhabitants stripped of their possessions until, in 1509, King James IV granted the Lordship of the castle to John Grant of Freuchie, holding him bound to repair the castle and equip it for the defence of the area.

After Flodden, in 1513, the castle was taken by the Lord of the Isles and the surrounding countryside again wasted. In 1527, the castle was in ruins.

The ruins which we see today are largely those of the castle as it was rebuilt in the sixteenth and seventeenth centuries. The early eighteenth century saw the building being plundered of lead and timber by the locals and, in 1715, a storm blew down part of the remaining structure.

Now in the hands of the Department of the Environment, the castle has received attention in the form of excavation and repairs.

KINCARDINE

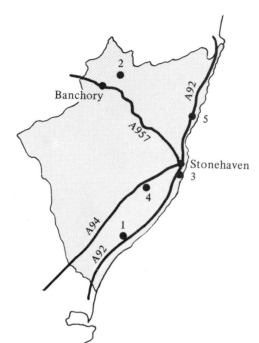

1. Benholm
2. Crathes
3. Dunnotar
4. Fiddes
5. Muchalls Castle

BENHOLM

Unsignposted and relatively recently ruined, Benholm Castle lies about a mile off the A92, between Montrose and Stonehaven.

The castle itself, a Tower House, has suffered greatly since the removal of its roof; the floors have rotted and fallen in and the upper levels of stonework are far from being safe. Built on to one side, the equally derelict remains of a large Georgian style house stand, roofless, floorless and stripped of everything which might be of value if only as scrap.

Peopled only by pigeons, Benholm Castle stands on private ground and should not be visited by people accompanied by children — the building is in far too dangerous a condition and the vaulted cellar of the tower house is used to store animal foodstuffs.

Opposite Page: Benholm castle.

230

Crathes castle, a fine example of the Scottish tower house.

CRATHES

A fine Tower House, administered by the National Trust, Crathes Castle, like that of Craigievar, displays many of the best features of the developed Scottish Tower House.

By the mid-sixteenth century the need for true defensive strength had become less intense than hitherto and builders were free to concentrate rather more on the aesthetics of their work, often producing buildings which symbolised military might without necessarily possessing that quality. All those impressive turrets, for example, to be seen on the upper reaches of castles of this kind were far more likely to have been put there for domestic uses, such as dressing or writing rooms, than for military purposes, though they were ideal positions from which to rake the outside walls with fire in the unlikely event of attack.

The massive-looking rounded corners of the building, however, have a practical purpose in that they were far harder to bash a hole in than the square variety, a popular method of storming a castle being to knock a hole in one corner in the hope that the wall would fall down, though, again, this would have been a most unlikely eventuality in the life of a Tower House, of this late date.

Although Crathes Castle, being administered by the National Trust, is rather more expensive to see over than those under the care of the Department of the Environment (and, indeed, than most privately owned castles, too), it is well worth a visit and the guide book, the work of Schomberg Scott, is both interesting and extremely informative.

DUNNOTTAR

Dunnottar Castle, standing on a strange high rock which rises from the sea about two miles south of Stonehaven, must be one of the most impressive ruins in the entire country.

Apart from the actual castle remains and the rock on which they stand, however, Dunnottar has great interest from a historical viewpoint, being the stronghold where the Crown Jewels and royal treasures, together valued at £20,000, were held against Cromwell's army in 1651.

A less creditable event in the castle's history was the imprisonment there, in 1685, of 122 Covenanters who were kept for over two months in such appalling conditions that many died and, when an escape attempt was made, a number of the recaptured escapees were tortured to death and others permanently maimed.

A splendid guide book is available from the Castle Custodian, containing such phrases as '... the event whose dark shadow is for evermore flung athwart the castle rock ...' and a great deal of old Scots quotations of almost undiscoverable (to the average English reader) meaning. Try '... Thai rewid nocht ws in to the toun off Ayr our trew barrownis quhen that thai hangyt thar.' and you will see what I mean.

Dunnottar castle

Fiddes castle.

FIDDES

Privately owned as a residence, Fiddes Castle is not open to the public, though the owners will permit the exterior of the buildings to be viewed by appointment only.

Believed to date from the late sixteenth century, the castle's history is associated with that of the Arbuthnot family who held the lands of Fiddes from the fourteenth until the eighteenth century.

The mid nineteenth century saw the castle disused except as a farm storehouse but, in 1918, it was bought and partially restored, this work being completed by Mr. Howard Johnson, the father of the present owner, who took great pains to ensure that the work was faithfully carried out in the correct style and manner.

MUCHALLS CASTLE

This is one of those small, delightful castles which, by virtue of its size has remained a charming family home.

The original castle, or Tower House, was incorporated in a later, seventeenth century building erected by Alexander Burnett of Leys. Open to the public from May to September on Sundays and Tuesdays between 3.00 and 5.00 p.m. only (bus parties by appointment only), the house contains ceilings whose plasterwork was described by the late Dr. Douglas Simpson C.B.E., D Litt. LL D, F.S.A., F.S.A. Scot. Hon. Frias, as 'the finest in Scotland.'

Muchalls castle.

KINROSS

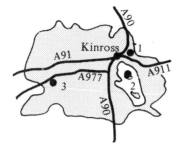

1. Burleigh
2. Loch Leven
3. Tulliebole

LOCH LEVEN

Seen from the M90 (or, indeed, the adjacent A90), Loch Leven Castle looks small and square and neat as it sits snugly amid the trees covering its small island.

Administered by Kinross Urban District Council, the Castle is open to the public who may be ferried out at regular intervals from a small landing stage on the town side of the Loch.

BURLEIGH

Rising from the right bank of the Burleigh Burn near Loch Leven, Burleigh Castle dates from the sixteenth century to judge by the Tower standing at the northern end of the site.

Of a somewhat later date than the Old Tower is a length of wall and another, smaller, tower which was more or less complete when the building was placed in the care of the Ministry of Works in 1928. Since that time, a considerable amount of restorative work has been carried out on the site to make it attractive and safe for visitors.

TULLIEBOLE

On the A977, just to the east of Drum and the Crook of Devon, Tulliebole Castle, the private property of Lord Moncrieff, stands behind a screen of trees and shrubbery.

Dating from the seventeenth century, the castle would, perhaps, be better described as a Laird's House, being obviously built very much with the comfort of its inhabitants in mind. In support of this, there is a panel above the door piece bear-ing a shield and the inscriptions

> THE LORD IS
> ONLIE MY DEFENCE
> 2 APRIL 1608

and

> PEACE BE
> WITHIN THY WALLES AND
> PROSPERITIE
> WITHIN THY HOUS.

Not open to visitors.

KIRKCUDBRIGHT

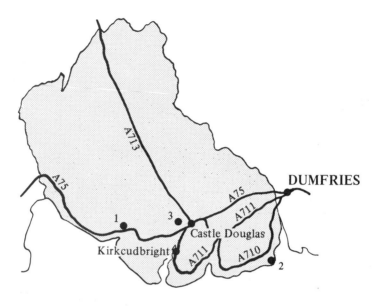

1. Cardoness
2. McLellan's Castle
3. Threave

CARDONESS

A short distance southwest of Gateway of Fleet, on the A75, this tall rectangular Tower stands on a one hundred foot mound rising directly from the roadside.

Built during the fifteenth century, the Tower is in a remarkable state of preservation, though the outbuildings which clustered round its south and east sides have gone. Apart from the condition and position of the Tower it is notable for the municipal nature of the flower beds which are cultivated around its walls and walks and for the incredible double-seater garderobe arranged in such a way that one celebrant sat above the other, his feet resting on the seat on either side of the person below.

The large, imposing, roofless ruin that is Maclellan's Castle dates from the late sixteenth century and is an outstanding example of the domestic architecture of that time.

Built by Sir Thomas Maclellan from stone taken from the old Royal Fortress which stood at Castledykes, to the west of the town, and from the Convent of Greyfriars on whose site the castle stands, Maclellan's Castle is said to have been roofless since 1752 — some sources maintaining that there were even rooms unused throughout the building's life.

Off the A75 and about two miles from the town of Castle Douglas, Threave Castle stands on a small island in the River Dee.

From the road and car park, visitors walk a considerable distance along a narrow, fenced track skirting several fields whose length is punctuated by twelve small gates of the kind that let only one person pass at a time. Finally, the path leads to the bank of a river where a bell summons the Castle Custodian, who rows across from a wooden jetty to ferry visitors to the island.

Built toward the end of the fourteenth century by Archibald the Grim,

Maclellan's castle

chief of the Black Douglases, the castle Tower stands four storeys high and is surrounded by a strong Curtain Wall with round towers set at the four corners. From the top of the Tower juts a stone 'gibbet' (probably a large corbel for supporting a machicolated platform over the entrance beneath) 'from which,' the custodian relates with relish, 'there was never a shortage of corpses hanging in the days of Archibald the Grim'. In support of his summary of the character of the wicked Archibald (other sources tend to present him as a just but ugly man) the custodian also points out the extremely unpleasant pit and prison cell in which unfortunate victims were thrown to suffer and, perhaps, die of starvation or 'chills'.

Owing to considerable restorative work, the castle is in a very fair state of preservation, partly a result of its having been used to house French prisoners of war during the nineteenth century.

LANARK

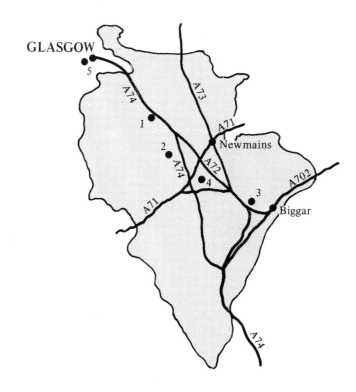

GLASGOW

1. Bothwell
2. Cadzow
3. Covington
4. Craignethan
5. Crookston

Bothwell castle engraved by John Slezer 1693.

BOTHWELL CASTLE

Bothwell is one of those rare castles in which the romantic charm of the ruin vies with the ingenuity of its defences as a primary source of interest.

Although no accurate date has been given for the building of Bothwell Castle, it has been authoritatively suggested that the latter half of the thirteenth century is most likely as the date of the original building, with repairs additions and alterations carrying on through to the sixteenth century.

Certainly the castle played a prominent part in the Scots' struggle for Independence, being besieged by them for fourteen months before falling at last out of the hands of the English. Two years later (1301), the English forces of Edward I recaptured the castle after a siege of less than a month, using a massive Belfrey (see chapter of siege engines etc.) which was made at Glasgow and which took two days and thirty wagons to transport it to Bothwell.

After Bannockburn, a number of English Officers took shelter at Bothwell only to be surrendered to the Scots by the Castle Governor. King Robert then dis-

mantled the castle and the English did not restore the damage until 1336, at which time they reoccupied it, employing John Kilburne (the master mason who was also rebuilding Edinburgh Castle) to direct twenty-six masons and eight quarrymen in the work.

In 1337, the castle once more returned to Scottish hands when Sir Andrew Moray, Warden of Scotland and the castle's rightful owner, captured and dismantled it.

Archibald the Grim, builder of Threave Castle, acquired Bothwell in about 1362 and, apparently, undertook the work of restoration for his arms appear in various parts of the stonework, much of which has been identified as belonging to the late fourteenth and early fifteenth centuries.

From 1455 onward, Bothwell passed from hand to hand as it was given by the Crown and then made forfeit as the various owners fell from favour.

Toward the end of the seventeenth century, Bothwell was acquired by the first Earl of Forfar who built a mansion to the east of the castle, obtaining building materials by pulling down parts of the ancient castle.

Some idea of the different families who have contributed to the building of Bothwell Castle may be obtained from the names of its different towers. Although, in recent years, some doubt has been cast on the assumption that the names given to the towers relate to their builders, a chronicler of about 1710 records that the castle has been built several times ' . . . as appears by the different names of Valence towr, Hamilton towr, the Cuming towr, and the Dungeon'.

Now property of the Earl of Home, Bothwell Castle is under the guardianship of the Department of the Environment and has been painstakingly excavated and repaired.

Standing on a rocky promontory in the valley of the Nethan, Craignethan Castle probably dates from the late fifteenth century when it was acquired by James, First Earl of Hamilton.

The seventeenth century dwelling at the southwest corner of the Courtyard is still inhabited but the late fifteenth century Tower at the east of the Inner Courtyard has suffered somewhat from the ravages of time.

Craignethan castle.

CROOKSTON

It is unfortunate that the state of Crookston Castle is such that we are unable to see much evidence of the arrangements made for defence.

There is a distinct scarcity of defensive firing loops in the central block and towers, so much so that it would have been impossible to adequately cover the walls in times of attack. We must therefore assume that the major defensive works were in the form of machicolations or other wall head devices.

MIDLOTHIAN

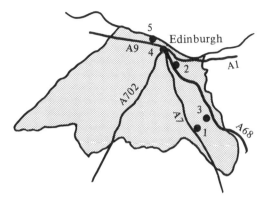

1. Borthwick
2. Crichton
3. Craigmillar
4. Edinburgh
5. Lauriston

This incredible Tower House, licensed in 1430, stands on the site of an earlier fortification known as the Mote of Lochorwart and is the finest extant example of the type of residence favoured by the Scottish Barons.

Part of its interest lies in its remarkable state of preservation and part in the way it illustrates the ingenious systems of defensive building devised to ensure the safety of the home team in the event of trouble with aggressive neighbours or worse.

Attackers (and, indeed, any visitors) could only gain access to the main building after first crossing a Drawbridge and passing through the Outer Gateway, which contained inner and outer gates in addition to a Portcullis, protected by a massive circular tower. Having passed through the Gateway, the Courtyard had to be crossed, passing two sides of the main Tower in the process, a flight of steps climbed to a parapet on the Courtyard Wall and then the Courtyard had to be recrossed by means of a bridge leading to the Tower Entrance which is on the first floor. Needless to say, defenders would not have remained inactive while attackers were performing these manoeuvres, firing upon them and hurling all kinds of unpleasantnesses from the heights above.

Although the emphasis laid on the defensive aspects of the building might suggest a somewhat barrack-like interior, this was, by the standards of the time and place, a remarkably comfortable and well appointed home. The huge fireplace, the screen which supported a minstrels' gallery, the buffet recess in which would be displayed the more valuable cups and dishes — all are evidence of the attention paid to domestic detail by the castle's builders. So well did they do their jobs, in fact, that subsequent owners never found the need to add to the original building for either defensive or domestic reasons.

The square Tower House, the nucleus around which the castle grew, dates from the later years of the fourteenth century and, by comparison with other, basically similar, buildings, appears to have afforded only rather primitive standards of comfort to its inhabitants.

In the early fifteenth century, however, additions were made which were fully abreast of the latest developments in castle design; a great Keep-Gatehouse was built to present a more aggressively defensive front to would-be attackers and, later in the same century, more buildings were added in such a way that the castle now occupies the four sides of a square enclosing a central Courtyard. Further alterations were carried out toward the end of the sixteenth century including the superb, diamond faceted facade on the north wall of the Courtyard which reflects the influence which his knowledge of Italy must have had on its builder, Earl Francis Bothwell, the 'eminently cultured ruffian' whose life was 'one continuous orgy of violence and uproar.'

Borthwick castle.

Crichton castle ,
Craigmillar castle,

CRAIGMILLAR

One of Midlothian's Big Three castles (with Borthwick and Crichton) Craigmillar stands as a near-perfect example of the best in Baronial building during the later middle ages.

Like those of the Tower House at Borthwick, the defences of Craigmillar are thoroughly thought out, taking full account of the topography of the site on which the building stands and providing for the use of cannon by the defenders. Internally, too the arrangement of stairs and the internal windows placed for observation of the passages clearly indicate that, even if attackers should gain access to the Tower itself, the battle would have by no means been over.

Dating from the late fourteenth or early fifteenth century, the Tower was equipped in 1427 with a massive Curtain Wall against the inside of which buildings were subsequently added, some of which date from the sixteenth century. In 1813, a human skeleton was found, buried in a dungeon by the Bakehouse in an upright position, from which Sir Walter Scott deduced that the owner of the skeleton must have been buried alive.

Other alterations were carried out over the years until, in the seventeenth century, the castle achieved its final state of development.

EDINBURGH

The great, rambling pile that is Edinburgh Castle is, like that at Stirling, a great disappointment to many visitors now that its days of greatest glory are long departed.

Large portions of the castle were destroyed in 1314 by Randolph, Earl of Moray, in accordance with the scorched earth policy adopted against the English by Robert Bruce and, apart from St. Margaret's Chapel in the Citadel, only the ruin of David's Tower is of earlier date than the fifteenth century.

The first reliable accounts of the castle date from the eleventh century when it was the royal residence of Malcolm III and his Queen, Margaret, who built the Chapel which stills bears her name. From that time on, Edinburgh was frequently used by Scottish monarchs though it would be some time before the city was made Capital of Scotland.

In 1174, Edinburgh Castle was placed in the hands of the English as part of the security demanded for the ransom of William the Lion by King Henry II but it was returned to the Scots following William's marriage to Ermardis de Beaumont, when it was restored to him and given as dowry to his new wife.

Time and again, throughout the troubled years of Scotland's independence, Edinburgh Castle changed hands — each change of ownership causing damage to the buildings and every garrison undertaking repairs and alterations.

During the Civil War, the castle withstood a three month siege before the Governor surrendered (some say treacherously). The last defence of the castle was brief and successful — Prince Charlie and his Highlanders marched on the town but, after a period of blockade, decided that they would be unable to take the castle with the limited means at their disposal. With the end of the '45, the history of Edinburgh Castle may be considered closed apart from the occasional State Visit.

LAURISTON

All that remains of a probable earlier castle on the site at Lauriston is the square Tower House which stands at the south-western corner of the existing house.

Left to the Nation in 1926, Lauriston Castle is preserved as an unlived in 'stately home', administered by Edinburgh Corporation as trustees of the former owners, Mr. and Mrs. W. R. Reid. Past owners include the famous financier, John Law, but the superb furnishings which are to be found in the house today were collected by Mr. Reid who was a notable collector and connoisseur of objects d'art.

Above: Edinburgh castle. Below: Lauriston castle.

MORAY

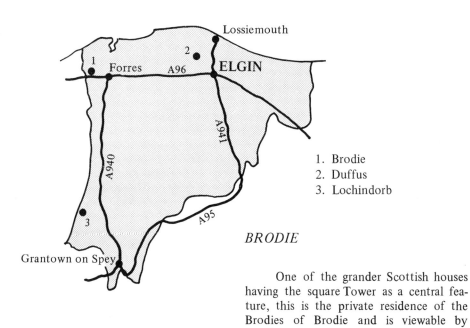

Lossiemouth

1 Forres   A96   **ELGIN**

2

A941

A940

A95

3

Grantown on Spey

1. Brodie
2. Duffus
3. Lochindorb

BRODIE

One of the grander Scottish houses having the square Tower as a central feature, this is the private residence of the Brodies of Brodie and is viewable by appointment only.

DUFFUS

In the relatively flat land to the north of Elgin, Duffus Castle, although standing on a quite low mound, is visible for a considerable distance around. Jackdaws circle and swirl round its ruined walls while, higher overhead, small jet aircraft hurtle and scream.

The original seat of the de Moravia, or Murray, family, this castle boasts a unique feature in its wide Outer Precinct which encloses eight acres.

The great stone Tower, unusual in that it covered no vaults and built about 1300, has slipped a considerable distance down the Motte, splitting in two in the process, and there are signs of subsidence to be seen elsewhere in the building, particularly in some of the window apertures.

Duffus castle.

Lochindorb.

LOCHINDORB

On an island in Lochindorb, this ruined castle can only be visited by boat and the problem lies in finding someone willing to act as casual ferryman.

The countryside here is wild and open with few roads or people and, although Lochindorb is not absolutely the most beautiful of the lochs, it is a quiet, attractive spot and ideal for those who really wish to escape from the regular tourist routes and areas.

Those lucky enough to get across to the castle will find that it boasts an unusual Portcullis Gate and no stairs. The fact that there are not even signs of there having been interior stairs suggests that the towers were probably ascended by means of ladders leading through trapdoors in the various floor levels on the way up.

Edward I stayed at Lochindorb in 1303 and it was probably he who was responsible for the building of the Outer Curtain Wall.

NAIRN

1. Cawdor
2. Rait

Cawdor castle.

Erected for the Bishop of Moray, Cawdor Castle was granted a licence in 1454.

The terms of the licence permitted the Thane to erect and fortify his castle 'with walls and ditches and equip the summit with turrets and means of defence, with warlike provisions and strengths . . .' but there was also the stipulation that the building must always be open and ready for use by the King and his successors.

Around the original, six storey building, considerable additions were made during the sixteenth and seventeenth centuries.

Dating most probably from the late thirteenth or early fourteenth century, Rait Castle has been described as combining the elements of 'Baronial pride and caution'.

An interesting feature is the existence here of a great, hooded fireplace – common enough in the Edwardian Castles of North Wales but almost unheard of in Scottish Castles of the period. It is not improbable that Sir Andrew de Rait, who, in 1304, was employed in a survey of the King's lands in Scotland, was responsible for this touch of grandeur in what must otherwise have been a rather spartan dwelling.

Rait Castle.

ORKNEY

Noltland 1.

WESTRAY

Kirkwall

MAINLAND

HOY

SOUTH
RONALDSAY

PENTLAND FIRTH

John'o Groats

Thurso

A836

A9

Wick

1. Noltland

Noltland castle

NOLTLAND

Noltland Castle is believed to have been built to the various designs of the infamous Gilbert Balfour as a fortress - hideout for use if and when things became too hot for him on the mainland.

Never completed, the castle is believed to have been left by him in much the same state as it is today, though it was besieged in 1592 and again, in 1650, when it was captured by the local Covenanters from a party of Montrose's officers who had taken refuge within its walls following their defeat at Carisdale.

PERTH

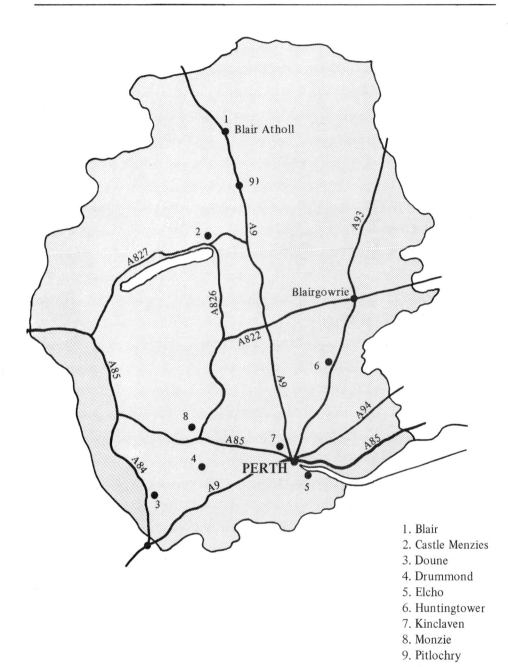

Blair Atholl

9)

Blairgowrie

PERTH

1. Blair
2. Castle Menzies
3. Doune
4. Drummond
5. Elcho
6. Huntingtower
7. Kinclaven
8. Monzie
9. Pitlochry

Blair castle

BLAIR

Blair Castle, 'the ancient home and fortress of the Earls and Dukes of Atholl', is a fantastic, larger than life stately home, beautifully maintained and furnished with the treasures and relics of centuries.

The oldest part of the castle dates back to the thirteenth century, though the building has been considerably enlarged at a later date.

MENZIES

More of a Strong House than a Castle, this fine building displays many of the better elements of the work of late sixteenth century Scottish builders.

Dating from about 1571, this is one of the earliest of the fully developed Z plan buildings whose great point of aesthetic interest is the contrast between the high, almost blank, walls with the wealth of movement and decoration contained in the massing of roofs, dormers and rounded turrets projecting from the upper corners.

Doune castle

DOUNE

Robert Stewart, Duke of Albany, Regent of Scotland and Earl of Fife, was a shrewd and powerful statesman and a clever strategist. It was natural, therefore, that when he ordered the building of a castle it should be situated in a dominant position. Doune Castle was placed on a site which commanded the two great mediaeval Scottish routes – one from Edinburgh to Inverlochy and the West, the other, from Glasgow to Inverness.

Built prior to 1400, Doune Castle is still privately owned and is considered to be among the finest buildings of its type and period remaining in Scotland, its design clearly indicating the degree to which treachery from within had to be considered by such powerful men as Albany, many of whom found it necessary to keep mercenary armies whose tergisative nature was evidently a constant source of concern.

An extremely interesting castle both to the historical scholar and casual visitor alike (note the very nice Yett with its wicket door), Doune is well documented in an excellent guide book, the work of the late W. Douglas Simpson, C.B.E., D.Litt., Ll.D., F.S.A., F.S.A.Scot., Hon. F.R.I.A.S. (who also wrote a great many of the guide books for those castles administered by the Department of the Environment). Not so much care has been taken, unfortunately, over the business of sign-posting the castle for those unfamiliar with the area, and navigators will have to keep an alert watch if the castle entrance is not to be missed.

First built in 1491 by John, First Lord Drummond, the old castle has been three times damaged by fire beside being besieged by Cromwell's forces in 1641.

Much of the present castle dates from the late seventeenth and late nineteenth centuries and, being inhabited, the castle as a whole has been modernised, though efforts have been made to preserve the character of the building. The grounds contain over thirteen acres of beautifully laid out pleasure gardens, largely restored and planted to a plan of 1830.

ELCHO

Apparently dating from the mid sixteenth century, Elcho Castle has had very little of its early history recorded.

The design of the castle is an indication of the way in which the strongholds of the mighty began to change from those whose purpose was primarily one of defence to those which provided a degree of home comfort to their inhabitants.

Just outside Perth off the A85 to Crieff stands a beautifully preserved Tower House.

Originally two houses, the alterations which made it one are still visible, though they are of sufficient age not to jar and, although the castle custodian lives in the lower half of one of the houses, much of the interior of the sections open to the public is as it was in the seventeenth century.

A particularly remarkable feature is the existence, in the Hall of the eastern tower, of an original, sixteenth century, tempera painted ceiling and beams and sections of the original painted plasterwork on the Walls.

From the outside can be seen one of the principal defensive features of Scottish tower houses; the entrance on the first floor, access being gained by means of a narrow ramp or flight of steps which would make the task of storming the door

Huntingtower house.

extremely difficult if not impossible.

The ancient seat of the Earls of Gowrie, Ruthven Castle saw brief fame during the Raid of Ruthven, when the young King James VI was kidnapped by the Earls of Mar and Gowrie in 1528.

KINCLAVEN

Originally the royal residence of King Alexander I, Kinclaven Castle was visited by Edward I during his temporary conquest of Scotland. Wallace, the great Scottish patriot took the castle from the English forces in 1297, shortly before the Battle of Stirling. The following year, he was defeated at Falkirk and taken off to London, later to be hanged, beheaded and quartered in the thorough manner of executions of those times.

All that remains of Kinclaven Castle is a ruined wall locked in a brambly wood on a knoll overlooking the River Tay, downstream of the southwestern end of Kinclaven Bridge.

The painted ceiling in the Hall at Huntingtower. Below: Kinclaven castle.

Monzie castle

MONZIE

At the end of what seems an interminable driveway, Monzie Castle proper is concealed from first view by the handsome mock castle which was built on to it during the nineteenth century.

The original fortified house, a private residence and, as such, not open to the public, dates from the early half of the seventeenth century and, although gutted by fire (along with the larger, nineteenth century addition) around the turn of the century, is in a splendid state of preservation, having been rebuilt internally by Lorrimer, the renowned Scottish architect.

BLACK CASTLE OF MOULIN,

Just outside Moulin, a small village to the north of Pitlochry, stand the few small remains of the once powerful Black Castle of Moulin.

Sadly decayed as they are, these ruins provide a clear picture of the typical plan of a castle of this type and period.

264

RENFREW

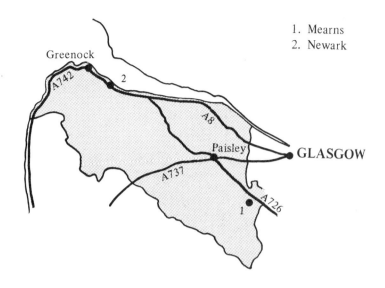

1. Mearns
2. Newark

Greenock

A742

2

A8

Paisley

GLASGOW

A737

A726

1

MEARNS

Mearns Castle was built by Herbert, First Lord Maxwell of Caerlaverock and Mearns, the licence being granted in 1449.

Commanding an excellent view over the Clyde Valley and surrounding countryside, the castle, a fairly minimal tower, was built for the defence of the local population and there is no evidence that its walls were ever breached.

Newark castle.

NEWARK

A stronghold of the Maxwells, who received the Barony of Newark in the early years of the fifteenth century, this imposing mansion began its life as a rectangular Tower Keep built about 1484. It was here that James IV probably stayed in 1495 en route for the Western Isles.

Originally consisting of Keep and Gatehouse joined by walls to enclose a central Court, the castle was later enlarged to include spacious apartments and the usual offices; this work being carried out toward the end of the sixteenth century.

ROXBURGH

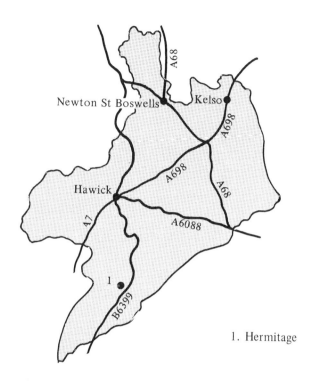

1. Hermitage

HERMITAGE

Standing neat and square, the ruin of Hermitage castle looks, from the outside, as though it lacks only roofs to make it good as new.

No precise date is given for the building of this castle, though records show that a Hermitage Castle was in existence in the late thirteenth century, Edward I ordering its repair in 1300 at a cost of £20. The castle as it was then would appear to have been demolished, for the oldest parts of the present building have been dated at around 1360 and clearly identified as being of the 'English Domestic' style.

The original castle changed hands repeatedly as the possession of Liddersdale

alternated between the English and the Scots until the widow of Sir William Douglas married an Englishman of the Dacre family who was probably responsible for the earliest part of the building as it stands today.

1371 saw the Douglases back in possession of Hermitage and it was they who built the great central block and, later, added the strong, square corner towers.

By the eighteenth century, the castle was in ruins but it was extensively repaired by the Duke of Buccleugh in about 1820 and is now in the hands of the Department of the Environment.

SHETLAND ISLES

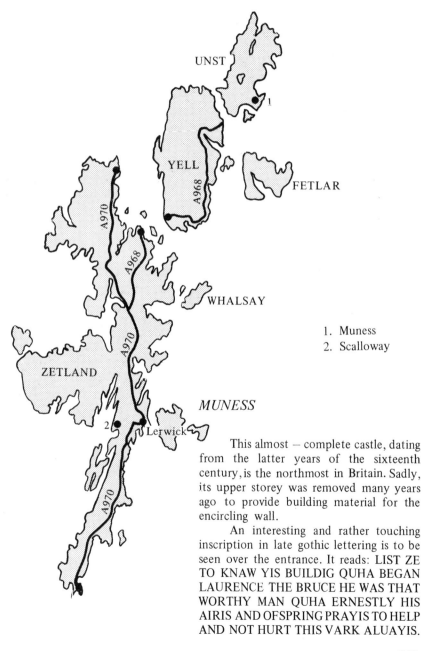

UNST

YELL

A968

FETLAR

A970

A968

A970

WHALSAY

ZETLAND

1. Muness
2. Scalloway

Lerwick

A970

MUNESS

This almost — complete castle, dating from the latter years of the sixteenth century, is the northmost in Britain. Sadly, its upper storey was removed many years ago to provide building material for the encircling wall.

An interesting and rather touching inscription in late gothic lettering is to be seen over the entrance. It reads: LIST ZE TO KNAW YIS BUILDIG QUHA BEGAN LAURENCE THE BRUCE HE WAS THAT WORTHY MAN QUHA ERNESTLY HIS AIRIS AND OFSPRING PRAYIS TO HELP AND NOT HURT THIS VARK ALUAYIS.

Muness castle

SCALLOWAY

Scalloway Castle was built in 1600 as a residence for the Earls of Shetland who, before this time, probably used Castle Strom, a few miles to the north in Lock Strom.

By 1703, the castle was neglected and fast decaying, much of the roofing gone and rain falling freely from floor to floor. Fortunately, the walls were so stoutly built that they survived long enough for the Commissioners of H.M. Works to undertake a certain amount of restorative work in 1908, ensuring that this fascinating building will remain for many years to come a source of interest to all who make the journey to see it.

Scalloway castle, c.1600

provide suitable accommodation for use as a Royal Residence, and certainly the distant view of the castle standing high above the town has a satisfactorily lordly appearance. James II made the castle a dower house for his Queen, Mary of Gueldres, holding a magnificent tournament there in the year of his marriage. Three years later he murdered William, Eighth Earl of Douglas within its walls, believing, mistakenly, that by so doing he would suppress the rebellion which he was convinced Douglas was planning with the Earl of Crawford.

1541 saw the birth of James III at Stirling, which remained his favourite residence until the time of his death in 1588 at Sauchieburn after being betrayed by his son, later crowned James IV.

James IV also spent considerable time at Stirling, improving the castle and its grounds until, refusing to break his league with France, he fought the English and died at Flodden.

His son, James V, continued the Royal tradition at Stirling, spending much of his childhood and married life here. James' daughter, Mary Queen of Scots, was crowned at Stirling and her son, another James, was christened in the castle and, the following year, was crowned in the parish Kirk of Stirling at the age of thirteen months, following the abdication of his mother.

With the establishment of James upon the English throne in 1603, Stirling's glory and importance began to diminish, it being used to imprison distinguished offenders.

Considerable damage was caused to the castle by General Monk for Parliament during the Civil War. He bombarded the castle for three days before a mutiny within caused the garrison to surrender.

Again, during the Jacobite risings, Stirling Castle saw some action but its great days were past and, although its buildings are still occupied, it is most unlikely that the building will ever be used either as a royal residence or fortress again.

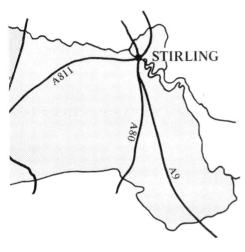

STIRLING

The towns of Edinburgh and Stirling have strong similarities; so do the castles, not least of which is the feeling of disappointed anticlimax which often possesses visitors to the two great fortresses.

At the time of Edward I's invasion, Stirling Castle was considered to be the most impregnable in Scotland. So strong did it prove when besieged that the English were obliged to increase the throwing power of their siege engines by stripping lead from the roofs of two Cathedrals and an Abbey. But, at that time, Stirling Castle was mainly a wooden affair!

The present castle dates from the fifteenth century, when it was altered to

Stirling castle today and as it appeared in the seventeenth century.

The Prospect of Sterling Castle

WEST LOTHIAN

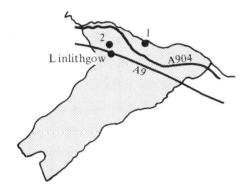

1. Blackness
2. Linlithgow

BLACKNESS

An important port in mediaeval times, on account of its proximity to the Royal Burgh of Lithlingow, there is, surprisingly, no mention of a castle here before the fifteenth century.

Used almost continuously until quite recently, firstly as a fortress, then a prison and lastly as a powder magazine, the castle underwent some modifications during its lifetime but it has since been restored to its seventeenth century appearance by the Commissioners of H.M. Works (now the Department of the Environment).

LITHLINGOW

A well-signposted, Department of the Environment administered, Royal Palace, Lithlingow was symmetrically built round all four sides of a rectangle and, although thick-walled, its character is quite clearly more domestic than military.

Edward I had the Peel built in 1301, at which time it was defended by palisades, and the oldest, still-remaining parts of the Palace date from 1400. The building as it stands today was completed under James V, the fire of 1746 being responsible for much delapidation.

Interesting from all aspects, the build-ing has virtually no roof though the first floor remains largely intact and there are some attractive details, such as the stone ceiling of the Queen's Oratory, and the incredible, sustained echoes in the wine cellar are a delight to children and childlike adults. The remains of huge fireplaces and the magnificent fountain in the Courtyard indicate again the domestic nature of the building (Mary Queen of Scots was born here in 1542) and the falling off of spartan living standards as a more peaceful way of life came to the area with the passing of time.

WALES

In Wales, as in England, castles existed before 1066, but the variety and abundance of building in the Middle Ages from the beginning of the Norman penetration to the Edwardian settlement after 1283 reflects a continuing struggle between those who wanted to invade Wales from across the English border and the tenacious established forces who wished to keep them out.

The difficulties experienced by the Normans in penetrating Wales can be seen in that, even twenty years after the invasions of England, the only castles known to have been built existed east of a line drawn from Rhuddlan, in the north, to Cardiff in the south. Twelve years later, in 1098, Norman infiltration of the north received a setback at the hands of King Magnus III of Norway who, operating by sea from the Isle of Man, defeated them at Caernarvon. They entered South Wales more easily however, and took over the lands of the established Welsh dynasties. These new Norman Lords, the families of the Welsh Marches, came to enjoy a measure of power and independence that, over the years, often embarrassed the English Kings to whom they owed allegiance.

Parts of Wales further north, however, produced a succession of leaders in the 12th and 13th centuries who were able to implant and continue national traditions despite efforts by successive English Kings to subdue them, often because they were able to take advantage of the latters' occupation elsewhere. Henry I often defended his titles abroad and even found himself in defence against a French invasion in 1101. The anarchy under his successor,

Stephen, allowed considerable sway to such successful Welsh leaders as Madog ap Maredudd. Another, Rhys ap Gruffydd, built up a national, rather than a provincial, state in the reign of Henry II despite having come to an agreement with the English King and also being his vassal.

By the end of the 12th century (Henry II died in 1189), there had been built in Wales over 100 castles, many of them on or near sites which exist as powerful stone castles today; Dolbardann, Brecon and Tretower are but three examples. William Marshall, one of the prominent personalities in Europe at that time, added to his important castles at Chepstow and Pembroke and, in the middle of the century, we find Henry III, another English King whose attention was drawn elsewhere, recognising Llywellyn ap Gruffydd as Prince of Wales — once again a concession to Nationalistic movements outside his control. Henry's difficulties in France and with the barons under Simon de Montfort gave the Welsh an unrealistic advantage which was quickly reversed by his son, Edward I, who put an end to Llywellyn's manoeuvrings in 1282 and those of his brother, David, in 1283.

Edward overcame rebellions in 1287 and 1294 and imposed settlement on the North of Wales because he gave his full attention to a complete strategy for this part of the country. His spectacular castles, mostly conceived with a fortified borough attached, were an integral part of the plan and the towns of Conray and Caernarvon for instance, at once strategic and administrative centres, ought to be seen by the visitor as a total conception. Indeed, these two, especially, remain so complete as to be perhaps the finest survivals of mediaeval fortified towns in Europe, despite the existence of such widely publicised examples in France as Carcasonne.

Edward's Welsh castles truly functioned as a tool for his domination of Wales but it is interesting to see once again how the process slowed down under kings who did not devote their single minded attention to it. The continuing military independence of the old Marcher Lords and the rebellion by Owain Glyndwr after the deposition of Richard II were part of a situation in which castles played an active and vital role, indeed Richard formally handed over the Crown to Henry Bolingbroke (later Henry IV) at Flint Castle. But it is also interesting that whilst, in England, castles continued to be newly built whose design reflected the changing needs of their owners, development in Wales practically stopped with the death of Edward I. He and his master mason, James of St. George, perfected the mediaeval castle in its ultimate form, linking successfully its dual roles in local defence and as part of a state scheme and, although castles in Wales were naturally modified or added to, we do not see the emergence there of new styles such as the Rectangular Castles of Bolton or Bodiam, Tower Houses like Ashby de La Zouche or Tattershall or the strongly fortified manor houses as at Kirby Muxloe or Herstmonceux.

Paradoxically however, the English developments are the fruit of such carefully prepared designs as Harlech or Beaumaris. The survival of these examples in such a complete state allows us to admire the great achievement of Edward and his designer in the fulfilment of their ideas. This is even better appreciated when one remembers that this single-mindedness in the construction of his great Welsh Castles exceeded by so much what Edward could afford that it nearly emptied the Royal Treasury for good.

BEAUMARIS

This beautiful castle was the last of the series built by Edward I as a means of holding the unruly Welsh in check after the defeat of Llywelyn and David, last of the native ruling Princes in 1282–3.

By no means the largest or grandest of the eight Edwardian strongholds in Wales, Beaumaris is in many ways the most perfectly designed, being a copybook example of the concentric castle which was, in its time, the ultimate in defensive building.

As explained in a foregoing chapter, the concept of concentric defence was to allow a defending force to retire, if necessary, from the Barbican or Forecourt to an Outer Ward and then perhaps to a Middle, then Inner Ward before, in extreme cases, making a final stand in the Keep or Donjon, each section being held as long as possible before being relinquished to the attacking armies. As an added defence, the Outer Curtain was built, as can be plainly seen at Beaumaris, to a lower height than the Inner Wall so that defending parties on both walls could fire simultaneously upon attackers outside the castle.

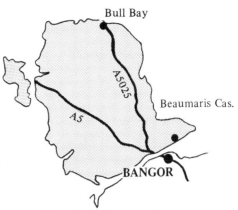

Apart from its attraction as a superb example of mediaeval military architecture, Beaumaris Castle cannot fail to delight the casual sightseeing visitor, its chequered walls rising from a reed edged moat making it one of the most picturesque castles in the country. Inside the castle, too, the building is of great interest, being just sufficiently preserved to allow the imagination to reconstruct its mediaeval splendour.

Here is a castle in which to spend some time, preferably armed with the guide book (published by HMSO for the Department of the Environment) whose author, Alan Phillips, M.A.(Oxon) clearly expresses and ably transmits his own delight in this splendid fortress.

BRECKNOCK

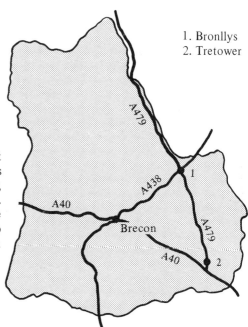

1. Bronllys
2. Tretower

BRECONSHIRE

Bronllys and Tretower both boast remains of Norman castles. The former is little more than a cylindrical, ruined Tower, fenced and rather overgrown but still high. Tretower's offering is similar but here the Keep stands within a circular Shell Keep and was used during the rising of Owain Glyndwr.

CAERNARVONSHIRE

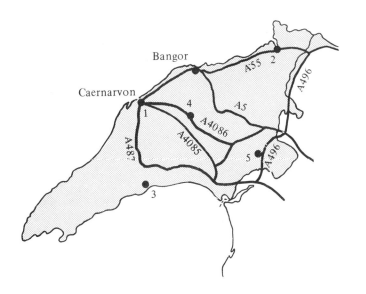

1. Caernarvon
2. Conway
3. Criccieth
4. Dolbarden
5. Dolwyddelan

Work commenced on Caernarvon Castle in the early summer of 1283 as the victorious King Edward I sought to establish once and for all his dominion over the unruly inhabitants of North Wales.

Planned, with the town of Caernarvon, as a single unit and administrative centre for North Wales, the castle rose swiftly, and when Edward and Eleanor, his Queen,visited the site in July the same year, they were accommodated in substantial timber apartments which had been prepared for their use. Returning in April 1284, Edward and Eleanor again occupied the timber buildings and it was doubtless in these that their son, Prince Edward, was born. By this time, the stone walls of both castle and town were rising fast and, by the following spring, much of the substance of the castle seems to have been well on the way to completion, attention by then being paid to the outfitting of the buildings.

Although the town walls on the south, west, and east sides of the castle were substantially built, the north wall of the castle directly facing the town was not treated with such urgency and when, ten years later, the Welsh rose under Madoc ap Llywelyn, they were able to breach the town wall and swarm across the ditch and low walls which were all that defended the castle along its northern side, burning all that they could including many of the records of the castle's construction.

Within a year, the English had regained Caernarvon, repaired the town walls and begun work on refortifying the castle, particularly on its townward side. Work continued for some thirty five years more however, before the castle had assumed a form similar to that which we see today and even then, parts of the castle were never completed; the rear section of the Queen's Gate, the Granary and North East Towers, all show signs that they were intended to be built against.

For some two hundred years, walled towns such as Caernarvon were closed to all

but English burgesses and, during that time, Caernarvon successfully withstood two sieges by the Welsh chieftain, Owain Glyndwr and his French allies but, apart from such minor upsets, both castle and tower enjoyed a period of orderly prosperity as the administrative centre of Welsh Government under English Rule.

When, under the Tudor Kings, the government of Wales was largely assimilated to that of England, Caernarvon (and the other Welsh Edwardian castles) became redundant and, by the mid-sixteenth century, despite the vast initial expenditure of money and effort, it was little more than a ruin, used only as a prison for debtors and other low felons.

Despite this, however, the outer walls of the castle were still intact and strong and the outbreak of the Civil War saw Caernarvon garrisoned for the King and thrice besieged. Following their normal policy, the Parliamentarians determined to dismantle both castle and town walls but, for reasons unexplained, this was never successfully undertaken.

The rise of the slate trade during the nineteenth century brought new prosperity to the town of Caernarvon, largely following the building of the railway there, and this, in turn, focused attention on the still magnificent ruin, causing restorative work to be undertaken on its stately walls.

Visitors to Caernarvon Castle are often surprised at the ruinous condition of the interior after first seeing the wonderfully complete exterior aspect. Despite this, there is much to see and a complete tour of the castle can be a lengthy and exhausting business, particularly for those who like to mentally test the effectiveness of the ingenious defensive systems which are such a feature of castles of this period. (The King's gate was furnished with five doors, six portcullisses, murder holes and arrow loops!)

Since the Investiture of Prince Charles as Prince of Wales in 1969, much additional interest has been created in this great castle and the Investiture Exhibition, in the North East Tower attracts many visitors, as does the Robing Room in the Chamberlain Tower.

The Queen's Tower contains a museum of the Royal Welsh Fusiliers which occupies three floors and there is a collection of armour in the Eagle Tower.

CONWAY

The great fortress of Conway stands as a monument to the conquest of Wales by Edward I of England.

Here, if legend is to be believed, the English King was served with the head of Llewelyn, last of the great Welsh Princes, in the Banqueting Hall though history, as usual, offers convincing arguments that this could not have been so.

Conway Castle was begun in 1283 and almost finished by 1288 at a cost which, translated into today's terms, approached £2 million. Its designer was the internationally famed James of St. George, from Savoy, and the best master craftsmen in the Kingdom, Richard of Chester, Henry of Oxford and Laurence of Canterbury, were summoned to Conway to employ their skills on the costliest Edwardian castle in Wales.

By the Christmas of 1290, Edward's Queen, Eleanor, was dead and buried in London (despite the plaque in the castle Chapel which states that she spent that festive season here with her husband), though the King did return here in 1294, when he was besieged by a Welsh force and was obliged to celebrate Christmas with a meal of salted meat, coarse bread and water sweetened with honey.

Despite the size and glory of Conway, it was not long before the castle began to fall into a state of gradual dilapidation.

Richard II arrived at Conway from Ireland in 1399. Here he met Bolingbroke's emissary, Henry Percy, Earl of Northumberland, who persuaded the King to ride to

London but, hardly had they left the safety of the castle when they were ambushed and the King taken to Flint Castle where he agreed to renounce the throne. Merlin had prophesied such an occurrence saying that '. . . there would be a King in Albion who, after a reign of twenty years, would be undone in parts of the North in a triangular place'. Conway, as old prints show, was indeed 'a triangular place' and certainly Richard was undone there.

During the reign of Henry VI, a group of Welshmen led by Gwilym the Rhys Tudor, proclaimed, from Conway, their allegiance to Owen Glendower. Besieged by Harry Hotspur, they held out for a time before yielding and being pardoned.

By 1628, the castle was in a ruinous condition but, in 1643, it was greatly re-fortified by the Archbishop of York at his own expense and garrisoned for the King against Parliament. In 1646, however, after a siege, the castle passed into the hands of the Roundheads who had greatly damaged it. 1665 saw parts of the castle being dismantled to be shipped to Ireland where the Third Lord Conway had other estates but the vessel carrying the materials was overtaken by a storm and sunk.

Little more is heard of Conway Castle until 1848, when the great railway bridge was thrown across the river and the L & NW Railway Company carried out some restorative repairs. The Department of the Environment now lease the building and it is they (and their forbears, the Ministry of Works and the Ministry of Public Buildings and Works) who are responsible for the generally well kept state of the castle as we see it today.

Conway

Close to the A947, Pwllheli–Portmadoc road, the ruin of Criccieth Castle stands on a high promontory overlooking both town and sea.

In effect, a castle within a castle, Criccieth dates from the thirteenth century when Llywelyn the Great, who ruled between 1200 and 1240, held captive here his son Gruffydd, and grandson, after Gruffydd had refused to acknowledge the supremacy of the English Crown. Later, Gruffydd's son, Llywelyn the Last, imprisoned another Welsh Prince (Maredudd ap Rhys, convicted of treason) at Criccieth, which suggests that the castle must, at that time, have been a suitable place for the imprisonment of important political figures.

In 1283, Edward I's armies had occupied Criccieth and in 1285 building work was in progress, possibly on the 'inner castle' which is believed to date from about that time. In 1294, two years after work had finished, a revolt broke out in North Wales and spread southward causing the English garrisons of coastal fortresses such as this to be virtually cut off from mutual contact except by sea. The strength of the garrison here at that time was twenty men, later increased to twenty-nine, though a number of townsmen and women are also recorded as having taken refuge within the castle walls with their children.

The revolt ended without incident here and, in 1286, the castle housed a number of Scottish prisoners taken during the invasion of Scotland.

1307 saw the first Prince of Wales crowned King Edward II and, for the next eighteen years, further work was carried out at Criccieth, both repairs and additions to the castle being undertaken.

A century of peace followed, to be broken by Owain Glyndwr (Owen Glendower) who rallied the Northern Welsh in 1400 and, with the help of a French and Breton fleet, cut off Criccieth and Harlech until both surrendered 'from hunger and despair'.

Burned and ruined, Criccieth was never restored until bought by W. Ormsby Gore, M.P. in 1858. Some repairs were carried out and, in 1933, Lord Harlech, a descendant, placed the castle under the guardianship of the then Office of Works (now the Department of the Environment) who cleared and excavated the site and who now maintain the castle.

Criccieth castle engraved 1742.

DOLBADARN

This ancient stronghold of Arfon stands at the northern end of the Pass of Llanberis, where it commanded the old route which ran from Caernarvon to the upper valley of the Conway.

Little is known of the story of Dolbadarn except that which can be gleaned from the minimal remains of the castle's walls; the circular Tower, the sole remaining building, dates probably from the time of Llewelyn Fawr, grandfather of the last undisputed ruler of Gwynedd, Llewelyn ap Gruffydd. The rubble built Curtain Wall dates probably from the later years of the twelfth century and other fragmentary remains of buildings suggest that they were added later.

In 1255, Llewelyn ap Gruffydd defeated his rivals in the struggle for Gwynedd and, it is said, imprisoned his elder brother, Owain, at Dolbadarn for twenty years. In 1277, Llewelyn was drawn into the final war with Edward I, losing life and land to the English King, and Dolbadarn Castle fell into ruins, being partly dismantled first.

DOLWYDDELAN

The ancient ruin of Dolwyddelan Castle, once a residence of Princes, stands small and rocky on a ridge near Bryn y Beddau — the Hill of Graves — where it commands the mediaeval road from the Vale of Conway to Ardudwy.

The oldest remaining part of the castle is the rectangular Keep, ascribed to the latter half of the twelfth century, to whose ruin roof and battlements were added during the nineteenth century, probably for the purpose of providing a romantic vantage point from which to admire the view.

Here lived Llewelyn Fawr, son of Iorwerth Trwyndwn, the Flat-nosed, when he ruled Gwynedd at the beginning of the thirteenth century, and here Edward I of England stayed after the castle was captured during his conquest of North Wales in 1283.

Now, small and isolated, the ruin is preserved by the Department of the Environment; a quiet, beautiful place for summer picnics and thoughts of dead heroes.

CARDIGAN

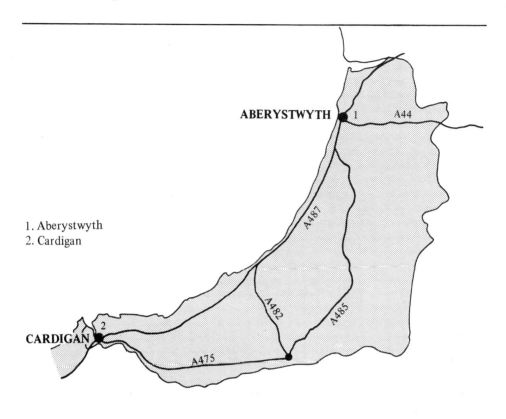

1. Aberystwyth
2. Cardigan

Built by King Edward I during his conquest of North Wales, this concentric castle dates from 1277 and stands on a promontory which, at that time, rose straight from the sea.

Five years after the commencement of the building, the castle was captured by a Welsh force led by Gruffydd ap Meredudd (a descendant of the Lord Rhys, who re-established the old Welsh Kingdom of Deheubarth) who again lost it to the English four months later.

From 1287 to 1295, the Welsh made several unsuccessful attempts to take the castle but it remained in English hands despite a siege lasting almost seven months.

The following hundred years saw little of dramatic interest at Aberystwyth until 1401, when the forces of Owain Glyndwr burned the town and attacked the castle. In the Autumn of 1404, Glyndwr's forces took the castle, holding it for almost four years during which time it housed the Welsh Chancellor and saw the ratification of a treaty of mutual aid between the Welsh and the French. In 1408, the English, under the command of Prince Henry (later Henry V of Agincourt fame), regained possession of the castle after reducing much of its structure with artillery fire.

During the Civil War, Aberystwyth declared for the King and a Mint was established in the castle to coin silver from the Cardiganshire mines, but this was later moved to Shrewsbury because of a blockade by land and sea. 1646 saw the surrender of the castle to the forces of Parliament, who destroyed it with gunpowder and left it in ruins which served thereafter as a stone quarry for local builders.

Cardigan 1610.

CARDIGAN

The date of the founding of Cardigan Castle is believed to have been 1092, Roger de Montgomery having done homage to William Rufus for the province of Cardigan sometime during the previous year.

It is most probable that this early castle was a simple Motte and Bailey affair and it was soon relinquished to Cadwgan ap Bleddyn, Prince of Powys, who assumed sovereignty of South Wales and held it until his death in 1110. King Henry I reclaimed South Wales but, in 1135, Gruffydd, eldest surviving son of Rhys ap Tewdwr, with other Welsh Chieftains, reconquered the province of Cardigan, defeating the English forces at the bloody battle of Crug Mawr just outside the town.

Several times the castle changed hands, twice being rebuilt or refortified by English masters and once by the Lord Rhys whose son, Gruffydd, sold it to the English in 1200. Again it passed from English to Welsh hands and back again several times, being reduced nearly to ruins by the forces of Llywelyn the Great in 1231 and rebuilt by Gilbert Marshall, Earl of Pembroke, in 1240, who is said to have improved its strength and accommodation considerably, building it, for the first time, of stone.

Beyond the fact that 'The Lordship, Castle and Town were settled by Henry VII on Catherine of Aragon, on her being betrothed to his eldest son, Arthur, Prince of Wales, as her dower', little more is heard of Cardigan Castle until the Civil War, when it was early taken for the King before being besieged by Parliamentary forces under Laugharne. This event is described in a letter from a Captain Richard Swanley to the Earl of Warwick thus:

'The castle being a considerable place, ably manned having the ordnance of the Convent frigate there shipwrecked, most obstinately held out, until a semi-culverine of brass, belonging to the Leopard, was mounted and played three days upon them, forcing a breach which was gallantly entered and made good by our party, and the castle stormed, wherein were 100 commanders and soldiers with their arms and good plunder, not forgetting the Convent ordnance, returned by Divine Providence ... The town and Castle reduced and the country in the major part as conceived, well affected. Our army are advancing towards Newcastle, the enemy's next garrison ...'

Now privately owned, the Castle is not open to the public.

CARMARTHEN

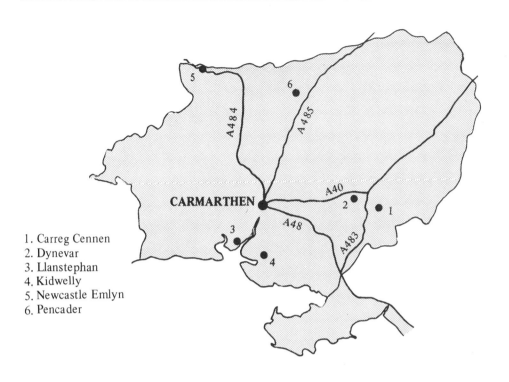

1. Carreg Cennen
2. Dynevar
3. Llanstephan
4. Kidwelly
5. Newcastle Emlyn
6. Pencader

CARREG CENNEN

Rising from the banks of the River Cennen is a three hundred foot high limestone crag on which is perched the castle of Carreg Cennen.

On a site which was possibly occupied in Roman times, the castle takes full advantage of its dramatically defensive position, the southern wall rising almost from the cliff edge on which it stands, and we are not surprised to learn that this Welsh stronghold, in the Kingdom of Deheubarth, did not fall to the English until the later years of the thirteenth century. It is from that time that most of the existing buildings date.

Taken by Owain Glyndwr early in the fifteenth century, the outbreak of the Wars of the Roses saw the castle in support of the Lancastrian cause and, following its surrender in 1462, the castle was slighted by five hundred men armed with picks and crowbars at a cost of £28 5s 6d.

An interesting feature of the construction of this ruined castle illustrates the changes in defensive building brought about by the improved instruments of siege which were being developed during the thirteenth century. Although the leading examples of this advance in castle design are to be seen in the great Edwardian castles of North Wales, here at Carreg Cennen we can clearly see that the defences were arranged almost as though destruction of the Outer Walls were taken for granted in times of attack; the second line of defended walls surrounding the Inner Ward; the elaborately defended, massive Gatehouse; the division of the castle into separate defensive sections; all are in line with the need to prevent an enemy from overrunning the entire fortress from a single access point.

Beneath the castle, a series of steps lead down from the Inner Ward to a cave of indeterminate purpose in which have been found remains of two adults and two children under a layer of stalagmite — possibly suggesting that the cave was in use during prehistoric times.

DYNEVOR

Llanstephan castle.

The largish, Round Keep at Dynevor is fairly low and minimal. It has been suggested that work was begun here but never completed.

LLANSTEPHAN

Llanstephan Castle, visible from the train, stands on a sharp headland on the Tywi Estuary.

Dating from the later years of the twelfth century, Llanstephan was one of the English castles which fell to Llywelyn the Great who, taking advantage of the distraction offered by the troubles arising out of Magna Carta, overran much of South Wales from his Northern province.

The fabric of the castle developed over the years, successive owners each contributing some addition or alteration to the structure. The castle changed hands many times during the period preceding 1482, frequently reverting to the Crown and being granted to this or that family. Strangely, at least four owners between 1377 and 1482 (including the young Prince of Wales, Edward V, the elder of the Princes in the Tower) were either murdered or executed and several others died childless.

Although taken and retaken during the various Welsh uprisings, Llanstephan Castle seems to have sunk into oblivion after the rising of Owain Glyndwr, never again being used for defensive purposes.

Used as farm buildings until 1860, Llanstephan Castle is extensively ruined, though there are some nice arches remaining, the whole being dominated by the twin towers of the Great Gatehouse.

291

KIDWELLY

Kidwelly castle.
Newcastle Emlyn opposite page.

Kidwelly Castle is one of these whose appearance and character seem to change radically with the angle from which it is viewed.

From the southeast, stark and cold, this is obviously a military, and militant, fortress. But, from the northeast, with the river curving away toward the spire of Priory Church nearby, the same towers and walls mass themselves differently, presenting a far more picturesque and romantic appearance.

Built early in the twelfth century, probably by Roger, Bishop of Salisbury, Kidwelly was soon embroiled in warfare with the Welsh rising which followed the death of Henry I in 1135 and, for over a hundred years, the castle repeatedly fell to, and was lost by, a succession of Welsh Warlords. It would seem that little, if any, building had been done in stone here prior to the latter end of the thirteenth century, the earliest remaining building being the square block enclosing the Inner Ward, closely followed by the Chapel and then the semicircular Outer Curtain early in the fourteenth century.

The line can still be traced of the perimeter of the old Walled Town whose fourteenth century Gatehouse can still be seen and, although the buildings within this area are all relatively recently built, it is believed that they still follow fairly closely the original street plan of the mediaeval settlement.

NEWCASTLE EMLYN

This castle, remarkable only for the relative uneventfulness of its life, stands quietly ruined on a moderately high, moderately steep, mound overlooking the River Teifi to the northeast of the town.

Local people express little interest in its continued existence, though it is a pleasant enough spot for picnics and serves well as the focal point for an evening's stroll with the dog.

PENCADER

Although marked on some maps as a castle, Pencader is certain to prove a disappointment to all but the most ardent castle-seeker.

All that can be seen of its remains are a few stones on a weed covered mound behind the schoolyard.

DENBIGH

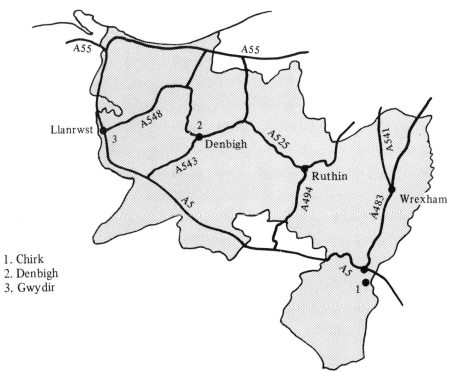

1. Chirk
2. Denbigh
3. Gwydir

CHIRK

Chirk Castle dates from the fourteenth century, when it was built by Roger Mortimer, Justice of North Wales.

For many years the castle changed hands with almost monotonous regularity until, in 1595, it was bought by Sir Thomas Myddleton, a merchant adventurer associated with Sir Walter Raleigh who made a fortune and was later elected Lord Mayor of London. The castle has remained the property of the Myddleton family ever since.

During the Civil War, the castle was seized by the Royalists while its owner (the son of Sir Thomas Myddleton, also Thomas) was away fighting for the Roundheads. Judiciously changing sides later in the war, Sir Thomas was granted, after the Restoration, £30,000 for repairs to Chirk.

Beautifully kept and furnished with treasures (including the Mortlake Tapestries) Chirk stands in some of the finest countryside that Wales has to offer.

DENBIGH

Denbigh Castle dates from 1282 when, after considerable resistance, Edward I captured the Hall of Daffydd ap Gruffydd, brother of Llywelyn, and granted the area to Henry de Lacy, Earl of Lincoln, instructing him to build a castle here from which the surrounding countryside might be kept in submission to the English rule.

De Lacy died in 1311, the castle uncompleted it is said because his eldest son, Edmund, was drowned in the well causing the Earl to leave and never revisit Denbigh.

The original building, in common with Edward I's policy, was a defensive wall round the town within which, at the best defended point, the actual castle itself was constructed later. Remains can still be seen of the old Town Walls and it is interesting to note that the present town of Denbigh stands outside them.

During the fifteenth century, Denbigh suffered rather badly, first from the rising of Owain Glyndwr during which the town was burned and, later, during the Wars of the Roses, when the castle was occupied by each side in turn and the town besieged and again burned by Jasper Tudor, Earl of Pembroke and half brother to the King. It is believed that the town was removed to its present site outside the walls during this period.

During the Civil War, the castle was held for the King, who stayed within its walls for three days in 1645, before surrendering the following year to the armies of Parliament.

After the Civil War, the castle was left in ruins until, in the mid-nineteenth century, a committee was formed to keep the ruins in a reasonable state of repair, doubtless as a tourist attraction.

Sadly, despite the attentions of the old Castle Committee and now the Department of the Environment, the ruins of Denbigh Castle are massive but somewhat unimposing, few buildings apart from the great Gatehouse standing to any appreciable height or holding any great interest for the casual visitor. Nevertheless, the great, lawned Courtyard surrounded by the ruined masonry is a pleasant enough place for a stroll and children, as always, will enjoy clambering about on the low sections of safe stonework.

GWYDIR

This charming mansion, dating from the fifteenth and sixteenth centuries, in no way merits the title of Castle.

Situated in pleasant gardens beside the B5106 road to Conway, the building was restored and furnished by the late Mr. Arthur Clegg who bought it in 1944 after it had been extensively ruined by fire.

FLINT

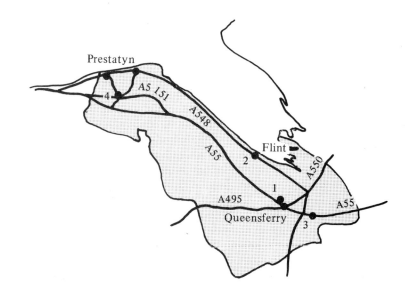

1. Ewloe
2. Flint
3. Hawarden
4. Rhuddlan

EWLOE

The ruins of Ewloe Castle lie hidden across a field and behind some trees close to the junction of the A55 with the A495.

Small and rubbly, the remains of this castle are nonetheless interesting and beautifully sited for tidy picnicers if not for mediaeval defence.

It is believed that the castle was originally established here by Owain Gwynedd in the mid twelfth century – the Welsh Tower is thought to date from about the end of the twelfth century – being either rebuilt or strengthened in the mid thirteenth century by Llywelyn ap Gruffydd after a period of English ownership.

After the completion of Flint Castle in about 1280 and the defeat and death of Llywelyn in 1282, Ewloe Castle ceased to have any military significance and little further is known about its history.

Now under the care of the Department of the Environment, the castle has been excavated and the ruin made safe, though children should be watched carefully as there are some inviting but unguarded walls. Not meriting a full-time custodian, booklets containing a brief history and description of Ewloe Castle are available at Flint Castle.

FLINT

Flint Castle was the first of the eight begun by Edward I during his conquest of North Wales, work starting on Sunday, July 25, 1277, and, following a practice he had learned in France, this castle was planned as part of a town, traces of which can still be seen today in the layout of streets.

The most remarkable feature of Flint Castle then, as now, was the vast, round Donjon built to serve as a last resort for a hard pressed garrison and as a flanking tower for the protection of the gateway to the Inner Bailey. Curiously, at the time it was built, this tower was some fifty years out of date but its strong resemblance to the Tour de Constance at Aigues Mortes (from where Edward set sail in 1270 on the Crusade which he undertook before returning to England to be crowned King) suggests that he was influenced more at this time by his French experience than by the more modern developments involving the system of concentric defence so well executed at Beaumaris (q.v.).

Certainly this great tower is impressive and, although only two storeys high, its walls are twenty-three feet thick. The circular, central chamber is twenty-three feet in diameter and surrounded by an interesting intramural passage to which it is connected by three openings. The well, situated in this passage, was so arranged that water could be drawn from it not only from the ground floor but from the floor above which housed the chief residence of the castle.

It was in the Chapel of this great building that Richard II heard Mass before leaving for London to sign his deed of abdication in favour of Henry Bolingbroke; Act Three of Shakespeare's Richard II graphically describes the scene for us.

Flint Castle played no part in the ensuing Wars of the Roses but, during the Civil War, it changed hands several times before being so thoroughly destroyed by Parliament that, in 1652, it was described as '... buried in its own ruins.'

The ruined stone castle of Hawarden dates from the closing years of the thirteenth century when it was built to replace an earlier, timber built stronghold which had been gained by Llywelyn with the help of Simon de Montfort.

On the suppression of de Montfort's rebellion, the castle reverted to the King who restored it to the Montalt family. During the Welsh uprising of 1282, however, the castle was stormed and burned before, at the end of the rising, being rebuilt of stone.

During the Civil War, the castle was garrisoned for Parliament but was taken by the Royalist forces who held out against a lengthy siege before receiving permission from the King to capitulate.

1647 saw the destruction of Hawarden along with the castles of Rhuddlan and Flint.

Now standing within sight of the relatively modern (1752-1809) Hawarden Castle, the ruin is well tended, its walks and wards planted with flowers and shrubs, where it graciously receives visitors on weekend afternoons through the summer.

Rhuddlan was the base from which, until 1063, Gruffydd ap Llywelyn harried the English as far east as Oswestry and Wrexham.

With the arrival of the Conqueror on the British scene, Rhuddlan was soon occupied by the Normans and, in 1073, a Motte and Bailey castle was thrown up, reputedly on the site of Gruffydd's stronghold.

This was the border country of the Wild West and, in the years that followed, Rhuddlan changed hands many times as the English strove to penetrate and subdue this corner of Wales. Finally, however, Edward I came to the throne of England and determined to consolidate his Kingdom, gathered a great army at Chester before establishing an advance base at Flint. From there he moved to Rhuddlan and, receiving the submission of Llywelyn ap Gruffydd (yes, there were two — Gruffydd ap Llywelyn and Llywelyn ap Gruffydd, not to mention all the other aps) set in hand the building of the castle we see today.

James of St. George was Edward's chief master mason for this castle as well as that at Flint. Later, as Master of the King's Works in Wales, he supervised the building of the castles at Harlech, Beaumaris, Caernarvon and Conway beside carrying out work at Lithlingow and other Scottish castle sites.

In 1278, the King stayed a week at Rhuddlan with Queen Eleanor and, three years later, the towers were roofed. 1282 was the year of the last Welsh Rising and in the following years sums of money were spent on repairing the castle which doubtless suffered some damage at the hands of Llywelyn's armies.

A workshop was built here for the Queen's goldsmith and 64 shillings were spent on red silk for pennants and royal standards for the castle.

Here, as elsewhere, Edward founded a town to go with his castle (despite the existence of a town there already) and, as at Flint, he protected the town with earthen banks topped by timber palisades. Here, too, in common with all eight of his Welsh developments, he took advantage of the proximity of the sea to provide for supplies to be delivered by ship, ordering a two mile long, deep water channel to be dug, into which the River Clwyd was diverted. This waterway was used by costal shipping until the nineteenth century.

The Statute of Rhuddlan, issued in 1284, created the shires of Anglesey, Caernarvon, Cardigan, Carmarthen, Flint and Merioneth and laid down the Administrative and Judicial structure for a large part of Wales which remained unchanged until the Act of Union of 1536. The Welsh nobles, however, were unwilling to ' ... yield to obedience to any other than a prince of their own nation, of their own language, and whose life and conversation were spotless and unblameable' whereupon the King promised them ' ...a prince who was born in Wales, could speak no English, and whose life and conversation nobody could stain'.

Upon their acceptance of this promise, the King straightaway named his infant son Edward, recently born in Caernarvon, who could certainly speak no English and whose life and conversation could be stained by no one. Seventeen years later, Prince Edward had the principality conferred upon him.

Not until the Civil War did Rhuddlan play any important part in the Nation's affairs when it was garrisoned and held for the Royalist cause until 1646. Two years later it was demolished by order of Parliament and for the next three hundred years served as a quarry for building stones.

The dominant features of the existing ruin at Rhuddlan are the twin round towers of the West Gatehouse and the wide, dry moat encircling three sides of the Outer Ward. It was to the Dock Gate by Gillot's Tower that ships would have brought their cargoes to the castle, berthing in the shelter and protection afforded by the projecting angles of the tower.

GLAMORGAN

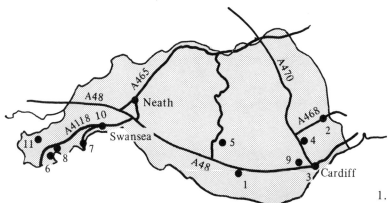

1. Beaupre
2. Caerphilly
3. Cardiff
4. Castell Coch
5. Coity
6. Oxwich
7. Oystermouth
8. Penricel
9. St. Fagans
10. Swansea
11. Woebley

Beaupre castle.

BEAUPRE

Not truly a Castle in the military sense of the word, Beaupre was a fortified house which was extensively rebuilt during the sixteenth century.

Associated from its earliest times with the Bassets, descendents of one of the earliest Norman settlers in Britain, Beaupre appears to have been built by a member of that family during the thirteenth century.

Little remains of the early buildings, however, and much of that which still stands is incorporated in the structure of the adjacent farmhouse (which is not open to public inspection). The fine, quadrangular building which we see, dates from the sixteenth century and was possibly built following damage to the earlier structure during the risings of Owain Glyndwr.

One of the finest of Beaupre's features is the seventeenth century porch of the Inner Gatehouse on the southern side of the Courtyard — generally acknowledged to be the finest of its kind in Wales.

CAERPHILLY

This great castle covers, including its water defences, an area of thirty acres, thus qualifying for the title of Biggest Castle in Wales.

Its incredible defensive system of walls, moats, dams and lakes is unique and the finest example of combined land and water defence in Britain, having been built by Earl Gilbert de Clare, Lord of Glamorgan who, after besting Gruffydd ap Rhys, the local Welsh ruler, feared an invasion from the north under Llywelyn ap Gruffydd.

In 1268, Earl Gilbert began to build a castle but, before work was finished, Llywelyn invaded the district and destroyed the work. Undaunted, the Earl began again and was again besieged by Llywelyn but, by the intervention of Henry II, a truce was called before the second building could be destroyed. Before a settlement could be reached between Llywelyn and the Earl, Gilbert forcibly regained possession of his castle and, with the aid of other local Barons, forced Llywelyn to withdraw.

It was not until the early fourteenth century that this fine castle rose to national prominence when its Lord, Hugh de Despenser, a favourite of King Edward II, became greedy and attempted to use his influence to hive off for his own use some of the land belonging to certain neighbouring Barons. Naturally this was resented and, in 1321, they rose and captured Caerphilly, only relinquishing their prize when the King led an army into Wales against them.

When, in 1326, Queen Isabella landed in East Anglia, the King fled to Wales, staying at Caerphilly for a few days before moving on to Neath. The Queen's forces besieged the castle through the winter of 1326–27 until, in April, the garrison surrendered on receipt of favourable terms, the King having himself been captured some five months earlier.

By the second quarter of the sixteenth century, the castle, having been neglected but for one Prison Tower, was a ruin and, apart from being slighted by Parliamentary forces during the Civil War, nothing more is heard of it.

Despite its lack of historical importance, Caerphilly Castle is an interesting ruin of which enough remains to make a visit well worthwhile; the lofty Eastern Gatehouse with its 'murder holes' and unusual chute serving a similar purpose; the leaning tower, its cant caused by an unsuccessful attempt at its demolition by Parliament's forces; the North and South Lakes connected by moats; all are sure to please and excite any who take the time to look and understand their construction and functions.

For those who like to be over-whelmed by conglomerates of extravagent artistic sugar icing, a tour of the interior of Cardiff Castle is heartily recommended but, if an hour seems too long a time to spend in being swamped by gold leaf ceilings, tiled, patterned floors, muralled walls and walls inset with precious stones, allegorical and mythological figures sprouting from every nook, cranny and mantelpiece, inlaid bronze doors, stained glass windows every-where, mirrored domes and decorated span-drels by the score; then stay away.

Cardiff castle.

CASTELL COCH

This must be, in its way, one of the most incredible eccentricities in the entire country.

Rebuilt, almost in its entirety, during the 1870s, Castell Coch is, externally, an extremely accurate reconstruction of a thirteenth century Welsh Castle of a type that is nowhere to be found intact. Its architect was William Burgess who, acting on instructions from John Patrick Crichton-Stuart, 3rd Marquess of Bute, transformed the neglected ruin of the original castle — uninhabited for over three hundred years — into a living building which, although possibly unsatisfactory from the point of view of the more meticulous academics, is certain to delight the vast majority of visitors.

Internally, too, Castell Coch is excit-ing for here we see the results of a collabor-ation between an immensely wealthy and enthusiastic patron and an eccentric but extremely well informed architect whose joint purpose was to create a masterpiece of Victorian mediaevalism.

Here is the decorator's art run riot; walls, ceilings, doorways and fireplaces all carved, painted, gilded and otherwise em-bellished with mythological and biblical figures, butterflies, stars and every other device which occured to the fanciful im-aginations of the Castle's creators.

CARDIFF

Cardiff Castle, standing on the site of a Roman fort, was begun toward the end of the eleventh century, when Robert Fitzhamon, Lord of Gloucester, led his private army into South Wales and threw up a Motte in the north west corner of the old Roman site. The polygonal shell keep, which is one of the few remains to be seen of the Norman castle here, was built on Fitzhamon's Motte sometime prior to 1158.

Gilbert de Clare rebuilt the Gatehouse Tower of the Keep in the latter half of the thirteenth century and divided the castle into Inner and Outer Wards by means of a great wall linking the Keep with the Black Tower. Following this, the conquest of Wales being accomplished, more spacious domestic buildings were erected along the castle's West Wall and these continued to spread throughout the succeeding years until, in the eighteenth century, the castle was very much as it is today.

Coity castle.
below: Oxwich castle.

COITY

Coity Castle, gaunt and windswept, stands about one and a half miles north-east of Bridgend.

After a period of fairly continuous building between the twelfth and fourteenth centuries, the castle was abandoned in the sixteenth century.

OXWICH

Situated by, and long used as, a farmyard, Oxwich is one of the most picturesque of the Gower Castles.

Rebuilt on the site of an earlier castle during the sixteenth century by Sir Rice Mansel, Oxwich replaced Penrice as the family seat. It is extensively ruined but some work is being undertaken by the Department of the Environment and, hopefully, it will one day be opened to the public for their safe enjoyment.

OYSTERMOUTH

Oystermouth Castle dates from the thirteenth century and stands at the top of a municipal park on the fringe of the town. In a moderate state of repair, it is cared for by the Swansea City Council and open at eccentrically random hours.

PENRICE

The ivy shrouded, late twelfth century ruin that was Penrice Castle stands on the western side of the Gower.

Enough fragments of walling remain to enable the perimeter of the single Bailey to be traced and the circular, Tower Keep still stands to a good height. The Gatehouse too, stands massively alone, guarding nothing against nobody.

Penrice castle and, above, Oystermouth.

ST. FAGANS

The thirteenth century Curtain of St. Fagan's Castle is still traceable throughout its length and it is from this that the present house here takes its name.

This is the home of the Welsh Folk Museum. The admirable purpose of such an establishment is to 'represent the life and culture of a nation, illustrating the arts and crafts, and in particular the building crafts, of the complete community . . .'.

The grounds contain a number of buildings, many of which have been transported here and rebuilt, to illustrate aspects of traditional Welsh architecture but, sadly, their vitality seems to have been lost somewhere along the way.

The late sixteenth – early seventeenth century house was built by Dr. John Gibbon who had recently acquired part of the Manor of St. Fagan's.

During the Civil War, the greatest of the Welsh battles took place in the Parish of St. Fagans, a Royalist army being routed by the Parliamentarians under Laugharne who took three thousand prisoners.

Swansea castle.

SWANSEA

Built toward the end of the thirteenth century, Swansea 'New' Castle stands to the south of the site of the 'Old' Castle which has long since disappeared.

Crammed into a row of shops and backed by a tall modern building, the ruin looks dirty and uncomfortable.

WEOBLEY

Reflecting the peaceful period during which it was built, Weobley is no great fortress from which to defy the world, though the scarcity and small size of its outside windows indicate that thoughts of defence were not entirely absent from the builder's mind. It seems that the building was erected to a series of plans, almost as though the design was trimmed and made less ambitious as resources ran low. Indications have been found to suggest that there was to have been an Outer Curtain enclosing a larger space within the castle and that other buildings were planned but never executed.

What it lacks in grandeur, however, Woebley makes up in charm and the relative completeness of its domestic buildings round the small open Courtyard form an interesting framework on which to build a mental picture of the day to day life of the inhabitants.

It seems fairly certain that the castle was built in the closing years of the thirteenth century and the first years of the fourteenth century, its owners being almost certainly the de la Bere family who owned considerable land in Gower. The only time it appears to have been involved in any military action was during the rising of Owain Glyndwr when it was attacked and damaged but, apart from that single instance, its life was so peaceful, that, by the fifteenth century it was described not as a castle but as a fortified manor house.

Generations of farmers lived here and, until quite recently, parts of the buildings were used to store farming implements.

MERIONETH

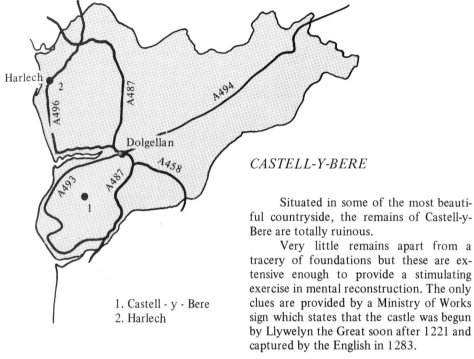

Harlech

2

A487

A494

A496

Dolgellan

A458

A493

A487

1

1. Castell - y - Bere
2. Harlech

CASTELL-Y-BERE

Situated in some of the most beautiful countryside, the remains of Castell-y-Bere are totally ruinous.

Very little remains apart from a tracery of foundations but these are extensive enough to provide a stimulating exercise in mental reconstruction. The only clues are provided by a Ministry of Works sign which states that the castle was begun by Llywelyn the Great soon after 1221 and captured by the English in 1283.

Harlech Castle stands above the town on a great crag overlooking Tremadoc Bay where it dominates the country for miles around; even the sea has yielded a half mile strip of land below the rock on which it stands.

One of the great works of Edward I, this castle is built on the concentric plan of defence of which Beaumaris (q.v.) is such a fine example. James of St. George, the veteran castle builder, supervised the work here as elsewhere on the King's behalf and Harlech Castle must surely be ranked as one of his great masterpieces.

For just over a century the castle stood virtually untried until in 1401, Owain Glyndwr rose against it causing one hundred men at arms and four hundred archers to be sent from Chester against him. By 1404, the garrison was down to forty men weakened by pestilence and desertion and Owain Glyndwr, who was trying to take Conway, returned to Harlech to negotiate the castle's terms of surrender.

Glyndwr then made Harlech his headquarters, installing his family in the castle but, in 1408-1409, the fortress fell to an army of one thousand men under Gilbert Talbot and his brother John.

This was a functional fortress, a symbol of military might and, as such, it contains nothing superfluous or inessential; every wall, tower, gateway and arrow loop was sited for maximum effect as soon becomes apparent during a tour of the castle. The enormous Gatehouse whose bulk dominates the entire structure, contained the principal apartments of the Constable of the Castle and it was so constructed that it could be effectively isolated from the rest of the castle — either as a last resort for a hard pressed garrison or as a protection for the Constable against mutiny from within.

The castle was built between 1285 and 1291 at a cost, in modern terms, of well over £1,000,000 and in 1294 it was besieged by Prince Madog who was repulsed by the garrison of thirty seven men.

During the Wars of the Roses, Harlech sheltered briefly Queen Margaret, on her way to Scotland after the capture of Henry VI at Northampton, before the castle was garrisoned for the Lancastrians; Dafydd ap Ieuan, Commander in England and Wales, being the last to yield to the Yorkists, which he did on August 14, 1468.

Despite ensuing years of neglect and decay during which the fortress, like so many others, was used merely as a Debtor's Prison, it again saw military service during the Civil War when it was gallantly held for the King against a lengthy siege before being taken and its demolition ordered. Fortunately, this order was never carried out and the building was allowed to moulder gradually until, in 1914, it was placed in the care of what is now the Department of the Environment.

MONMOUTH

1. Caldicot
2. Chepstow
3. Grosmont
4. Newport
5. Raglan
6. Skenfrith
7. White

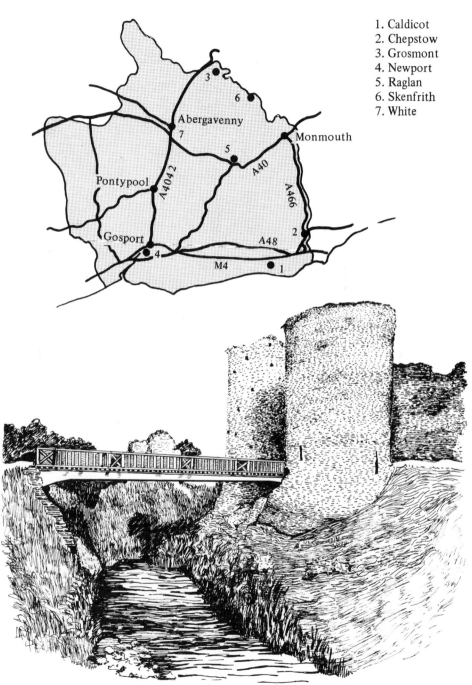

CALDICOT

Caldicot Castle is an extensive and very impressive ruin.

Based on an earlier, eleventh century, fortification, the castle was extended and converted into a magnificent stone fortress by the de Bohun family, Earls of Hereford, who held it until 1377. The twelfth century has been given as the period during which most of this work was carried out, though it continued well into the thirteenth century and the Gatehouse dates from the fourteenth century.

With the failure of the Bohun line, the castle passed, eventually to the Dukes of Buckingham the third of whom was a victim of the jealousy of Henry VIII. By 1613, we are told, Caldicot Castle was a total ruin.

The Gatehouse has subsequently been restored as a noble residence.

Caldicot castle.

CHEPSTOW

Chepstow was one of the first stone castles to have been built after the Norman Conquest of Britain, and much of the original building survives — notably the Great Tower which stands between the Upper and Middle Baileys.

Earl William Marshall married Isabel, heiress of Chepstow and of Pembroke (q.v.) Castles, and instituted extensive building programmes for both fortresses, the work at Chepstow being continued after his death by his sons. Further important additions were made to the building by William Marshall's great grandson, Roger Bigod III, including a new range of domestic buildings in the Lower Bailey, Marten's Tower, and additions to the original Great Tower.

The castle came into the hands of William Herbert, master of Raglan (q.v.), in 1468 and, for a time, the fortunes of the two castles followed similar lines, though Chepstow was surrendered far more readily than Raglan during the First Civil War. During the Second Civil War, the castle was again held for the King, being taken after a siege by Cromwell en route to Pembrokeshire. Unlike most Royalist fortresses, this was not destroyed after its capture, but was given to Cromwell, repaired and garrisoned. After the restoration, the castle was kept garrisoned and used as a prison for such figures as Henry Marten, the regicide, who gave his name to the tower in which he spent twenty years' comfortable captivity.

The ruin of Chepstow Castle is picturesquely sited on a ridge close to the River Wye. Long and narrow in plan, the castle walls contain three Baileys set side by side with Gatehouses at both upper and lower ends; a somewhat unusual plan dictated by the contours of the ground on which it stands.

Chepstow castle.

GROSMONT

One, with White Castle and Skenfrith, of the Three Castles which controlled the area from the Black Hills to the River Wye, Grosmont Castle had a relatively short useful lifespan of little over two centuries.

Built during the early years of the thirteenth century, the castle saw some importance during the Welsh risings and changed hands several times on the orders of the Crown as successive holders fell from favour or died.

Here it was that, after raising a siege which was being conducted by the combined forces of Llywelyn, Richard Marshall and Hubert de Burgh (a former owner of Grosmont) the King's army camped, to be surprised in the night by a large party of the enemy's horse soldiers who slew many of the King's soldiers sleeping in trenches outside the castle walls before carrying off '. . . 500 horses, besides waggons, provisions, and much treasure'.

Later, in 1405, Owain Glyndwr was defeated here by Henry, Prince of Wales, later to become Henry V.

After the accession of King Edward IV, Grosmont, with other Lancastrian castles, was dismantled, its period of usefulness over and the minimal ruins which remain have, apart from some excavation and restoration by the Ministry of Public Buildings and Works (now the Department of the Environment) altered little from that time to this.

314

The Norman castle at Newport was built during the twelfth century to guard the crossing of the River Usk and it was one of the many castles in Wales raided and burnt by Owain Glyndwr, being finally destroyed in the latter stages of the Civil War by troops under Oliver Cromwell.

Little of the original castle still remains on the bank of the Usk beside the main Newport Bridge and much of its dignity was lost during the nineteenth century when it was joined with other buildings, its South Tower being used to manufacture nails and the other tower constituting part of a Brewery.

More recently the grassed area next to the castle has provided a pleasant spot for relaxation for Newport shoppers and office workers during their lunch hour or at week-ends. However the first stage of a new ring road through Newport now overshadows the future of the area, although the castle itself, under the Department of the Environment, will remain.

Newport castle.

The massive, angular ruin of Raglan Castle dates from the fifteenth century and stands on the site of what was probably a twelfth, or even eleventh, century Motte and Bailey fortification.

During the fifteenth century, Might was Right to an alarming degree and many of the wealthy and aristocratic families consolidated their positions by force of arms — frequently employing considerable private armies to this end. William ap Thomas seems to have been such a man for we are told that, when a dispute arose over the appointment of a new Prior at Goldcliff, he provided the claimant to the office with a group of eighty armed men who carried off the rival Prior and chained him up in Usk, where Sir William forced him to resign.

A man who buys the loyalty of soldiers must always be prepared for a rival to outbid his price and the plan of Raglan Castle shows that Sir William was fully aware of this fact. The moat encircled Great Tower, self contained and

immensely strong, was a fortress from which to conduct a final stand against attackers from without or against treachery from within.

Sir William died soon after his Great Tower was built and it fell to his son and heir, William Herbert to continue the building of Raglan Castle.

Some two years after his father's death, Sir William Herbert was outlawed for 'the mischief and grievance he has brought upon the king's liege subjects in diverse parts, robbing some of them, beating and maiming some, and causing the death of many', though shortly after, we are told, he had his 'Lyfe graunted, and godes, so he make amendys to theym he hath offended.'

Largely instrumental in the victory of the Yorkists in the Wars of the Roses, having at his own cost raised the greater part of the victorious army, Herbert was naturally in line for considerable advancement under Edward IV. Honours were heaped upon him and, in 1468, he was created Earl of Pembroke.

Raglan was William Herbert's home and the centre of his power, it is not surprising, therefore, that the castle he built should be of a size and grandeur to reflect his power and wealth. Unfortunately for him, however, he with his brother Richard and other prominent Welshmen, was beheaded two years later at Northampton, following the defeat of his army at the Battle of Edgecote.

During the Elizabethan age, further building was carried out at Raglan, notably the Long Gallery with its great bow window, and upper parts of the Gatehouse range and Buttery. It is difficult now for the imagination to furnish the bleak walls of Raglan with the rich decoration of this period, but some small idea of the interior may be obtained from the chimney piece and sections of wall panelling which were removed from Raglan to Badminton on the destruction of this great castle after the Civil War.

The Earl of Worcester, then owner of Raglan castle, garrisoned the Castle for the King at a reputed cost of £40,000 to himself, while his son, Lord Herbert, who was the King's Lieutenant General in South Wales, received and passed on to the Royalist cause further sums of money said to have totalled almost £1,000,000.

Besieged by some 3,500 men under Sir Thomas Fairfax, Colonel Morgan and Parliament's most skilful siege engineer, Captain Hooper, the garrison were at last forced into submission, their surrender marking the end of the first Civil War.

The castle was plundered and largely dismantled by hand after its surrender and, although it was later restored to the family, it was never rebuilt, being replaced by a new family mansion at Badminton.

SKENFRITH

The Castle of Skenfrith, standing on the west bank of the River Monmow, comprises the two basic elements of defensive buildings; a Curtain Wall with a free standing round Tower in the space it encloses.

Certainly there were once other stone buildings contained within the safety of the Curtain for their foundations and lower courses are to be seen along both eastern and western sides of the Ward and we are told that King Henry III was here in September 1221 and again in August 1222,

Opposite: Raglan castle.

Below: Skenfrith.

the castle at that time being in the possession of Hubert de Burgh, Justiciar of England and Earl of Kent, a man of considerable influence.

Almost certainly, the whole of Skenfrith Castle as we see it today (with the exception only of one central tower added later to the West Curtain) was built by Hubert de Burgh to replace an earlier fortification which was almost certainly of timber and earth. Its history is closely allied to that of Grosmont and White Castle, the three becoming known as The Three Castles, which together commanded an area from the Black Mountains to the Wye through which ran the three main east-west routes.

With Grosmont and White Castle, Skenfrith was kept fortified through the years of the Welsh Risings under Llywelyn the Great and his grandson. Llywelyn ap Gruffyd, but, after this time, Skenfrith ceased to be of strategic importance and, by the sixteenth century, it is believed to have been in ruins.

WHITE CASTLE

Probably so named from the white plaster with which its exterior walls were covered, White Castle is the oldest, largest and most picturesque of the ruins comprising the Three Castles (see also Skenfrith and Grosmount).

Dating from about the middle of the twelfth century there was a stone tower here, which was demolished during the thirteenth century, and the later years of the twelfth century saw the erection of the Inner Curtain Wall which stands to this day.

Of prime importance during the Welsh Risings, White Castle continued to be of consequence in the immediate years which followed, when it served as an administrative centre for the area and a place where levies were mustered for the Scottish wars.

Ruined by the sixteenth century, White Castle is now in the hands of the Department of the Environment, under whose guardianship it has been excavated and partly repaired beside being enhanced as a beauty spot by the clearing of the moat whose tree lined banks make this a popular spot with summer visitors.

318

MONTGOMERY

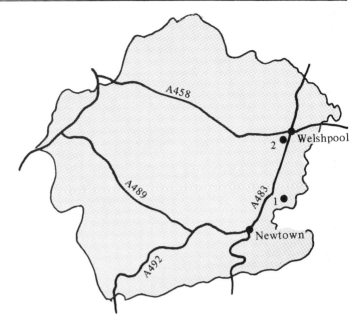

1. Montgomery
2. Powis

MONTGOMERY

The ruins of Montgomery Castle, dating from the thirteenth century, stand on a hill high above the town which, although nominally the County Town, is little more than a village.

Ivy grown in parts but generally cleared and cleaned up for the benefit of visitors, the castle is in an extremely ruinous condition though some walls stand to a fair height still.

The castle was for many years the home of the Herbert family one of whom, George Herbert, was the widely known Clergyman-poet.

POWIS

A property of the National Trust, Powis Castle stands just to the south of Welshpool.

The castle, which has been continuously inhabited for over five hundred years, is fat towered, well preserved and stuffed to the roof with treasures including tapestries, furniture, paintings and relics of Clive of India.

Surrounding the castle are some very fine terraced gardens dating from the eighteenth century and other stretches of tree studded lawn which prove extremely popular with summer visitors.

PEMBROKESHIRE

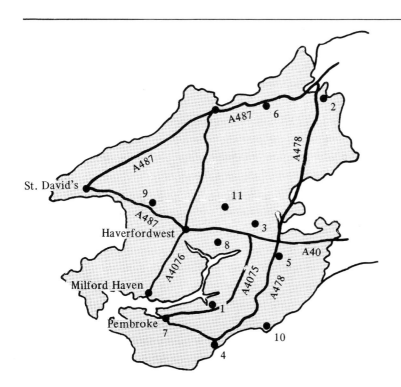

1. Carew
2. Cilgarren
3. Llawhaden
4. Manorbier
5. Narberth
6. Newport
7. Pembroke
8. Picton
9. Roch
10. Tenby
11. Wiston

CAREW CASTLE

Only six miles from the popular Pembrokeshire resort of Tenby, Carew Castle was once one of the royal demesnes of the Princes of South Wales.

Ivy grown, ruined, this castle is pervaded by an air of melancholy charm which, in spite of the massiveness of its walls and towers, is somehow feminine — the feeling being particularly strong in the grassy Courtyard where the shell of the building seems all light and air and quite unmilitary.

We first hear of this castle when it was given by Rhys ap Tewdwr to Gerald de Windesor (given the Lordship here by Henry I) as part of the marriage portion of his daughter, Nest, a woman so beautiful that she has become known as the Helen of Wales. (The story goes that Nest had been held hostage by Henry I against her father's good behaviour and had been seduced by the King who then arranged her marriage to Gerald partly as a means of ensuring good relationships with the Princes of South Wales.) At this time, of course, the castle was not as we see it today, for the earliest part of the building, the Old Tower, dates probably from the late twelfth or early thirteenth century (possibly having been built by the son of Gerald and Nest, William, who assumed the name Carew), and the other buildings were all added at later dates.

The North Front of the building, obviously domestic in character, dates from the late sixteenth century when Sir John Perrot rebuilt it in grand style in the hope (it is said) of entertaining Queen Elizabeth I there. We are told that Sir John fell from favour and left this work unfinished, the castle returning, on his attainder, to the Carew family whose descendants have owned it ever since.

CILGERRAN

Despite early Norman incursions into South Wales, it was not until the reign of Henry I (1100–1135) that the Lordship of Cilgerran was established and held by Gerald de Windesor.

Remains of five Motte and Bailey castles are to be found in the old Cantref of Emlyn, in which Cilgerran stands, one of which was known as Cenarth Bychan. It may have been Cilgerran or, indeed, any of the others, but, since the weight of opinion seems to be on the side of Cilgerran, we may perhaps assume that it was from these walls in 1109 that Cadwgan ap Bleddyn carried off the beautiful Nest, wife of Gerald de Windesor, after seeing and becoming infatuated with her at an Eisteddfod in nearby Cardigan.

In 1164, the Lord Rhys, a grandson of Rhys ap Tewdwr (Nest's father) re-established the old Kingdom of Deheubarth, capturing first Cardigan, then Cilgerran in the process, finally coming to terms with the English King who recognised his position as ruler in Deheubarth. On Rhys's death, however, the Kingdom fell apart and Cilgerran was captured by William Marshall, later Earl of Pembroke, who soon lost it to Llewelyn the Great, the hero Prince of North Wales.

Eight years later, William Marshall's son, also William, retook Cilgerran and rebuilt it, the two great circular Towers which still survive probably dating from this time.

Despite the efforts in 1257 of Llewelyn ap Gruffydd, who ravaged the surrounding countryside and beat the English in a battle fought nearby, Cilgerran did not fall again into Welsh hands for many years.

With the death of Llewelyn in 1283, Welsh independence was at an end and neighbouring Emlyn became a Crown Lord ship, severing connections with Cilgerran and leading to the eventual acceptance of the River Cych as the boundary between the counties of Pembrokeshire and Carmarthanshire.

In 1245, Cilgerran became part of the Lordship of Abergavenny until, in 1339, the holder of Cilgerran was created Earl of Pembroke, thus bringing the castle back to its original fold.

Having fallen into a state of serious disrepair between 1245 and 1372, Cilgerran castle was virtually ignored until a French invasion was feared and, in 1377, King Edward III ordered its repair.

At the height of Owain Glyndwr's revolt, in 1405, the castle was again occupied briefly by Welsh forces who reputedly laid it waste.

The Wars of the Roses saw the castle change hands several times but there are no accounts of it having been actively concerned with the Civil War.

By the end of the eighteenth century, the ruins of Cilgerran Castle were visited by groups of tourists, a practice which has continued since.

Llawhaden castle.

Llawhaden, one of the richest possessions of the Bishops of the See of St. David's, was protected during the twelfth century by a Ring Motte castle containing, doubtless, timber buildings which would have formed the Bishop's Residence.

Captured and razed by the Lord Rhys in 1192, the castle's defences were probably rebuilt of stone when the Bishop recovered his property. It was in 1280, however, when Thomas Bek was elected Bishop, that a period of lavish expenditure began on the chosen residences of Bishops and it is from a period just after this that the present castle of Llawhaden sprang.

The ruin that we see rising protectively above nearby houses today dates from the early fourteenth century and was probably the work of Bishop David Martin, Bek's successor. The Gatehouse, the only significant later addition, was built during the latter part of the fourteenth century and still stands to its full height.

Dismantled by Bishop Barlow in the second quarter of the sixteenth century, the castle served for many years as a quarry from which local builders helped themselves until, in the latter years of the nineteenth century, the ruin was cared for by the Ancient Monuments Committee for Pembrokeshire.

MANORBIER

This privately owned castle stands flower grown and smooth lawned looking down where the '. . . Severn Sea, bending its course to Ireland, enters a hollow bay . . .'.

The birthplace and home of Giraldus Cambrensis (Gerald of Wales), Manorbier dates from the twelfth century when Odo de Barri held the Lordship here under Gerald de Windesor, whose name is associated with all the castles locally. Odo's son, William, married Anghared, daughter of Gerald de Windesor and Nest, thus cementing the friendly relationship between the two families, and from Manorbier the sons of William and Anghared joined the conquest of Ireland, the Barry families of Ireland being descended from their stock.

Particularly interesting features of Manorbier in its present state are the rooms set aside to display the Portcullis winding gear and the workplace of Gerald of Wales where his effigy is shown seated at a rude table in surroundings as nearly as possible like those in which he actually worked.

The majority of the castle buildings which remain were erected by William de Barri, Gerald's father, only a few minor alterations having been made since 1300. It was fortified against Owain Glyndwr and again during the Civil War, when it was captured in 1645 by the Parliamentary forces under Rowland Laugharne.

Narberth castle.

Newport castle.

NARBERTH

The rambling, overgrown ruins of Narberth castle lie just to the south of the quiet town, unexcavated and unrestored, where they have served the local builders for centuries as a source of stone for building purposes.

Probably built in the twelfth century, Narberth Castle was taken and destroyed by Llewelyn the Great since when it seems to have remained a ruin.

NEWPORT

Just off the A487, coast road, between Fishguard and Cardigan, Newport Castle suddenly appears above the trees at the top of a steep hill.

Not much of the original structure remains (and later additions are used as a guest house) though garden and grounds contain fragmentary parts of the old castle, including a small stone Dungeon, discovered during the last century, which bears a Welsh inscription giving details of its discovery.

PEMBROKE

This huge fortress with its unique round Great Keep is undoubtedly the finest in the county of Pembrokeshire and stands on a site which may well have been fortified since Roman times.

The present castle was begun in 1093, when Arnulph de Montgomery fortified the site against the Welsh and placed it in the custody of Gerald de Windesor who successfully resisted the attacks of Cadwgan ap Bleddyn (who later captured Gerald's wife, the beautiful Nest, at Cilgerran Castle q.v.).

In 1138, the Earldom of Pembroke was created and Gilbert de Clare (surname Strongbow) was the first of the succession of nobles to hold the position, enlarging and strengthening the castle to make it a fit place for a man of his high rank. Gilbert's son, Richard Strongbow, was the conqueror of Ireland, using Pembroke Castle as his base during the Irish Wars and, on his death in 1176, his daughter and heiress, Isabel, passed with his estates into the hands of King Henry II who later married her to William Marshall, Earl of Pembroke

and builder of the Great Keep and Norman Hall. William was cursed by the Irish Bishop of Ferns, who accused him of robbing him of two manors, declaring that all his sons should die childless. This prophecy came true causing Pembroke Castle eventually to pass to William's second daughter, Joan, who married the great English Baron, Warine de Munchensy, a man who made further additions to the castle buildings.

During the Wars of the Roses, Pembroke Castle changed hands several times before seeing a time of peace and uneventfulness which lasted until the Civil Wars.

During the early phases of the great struggle between the Royalist and Parliamentarian forces, Pembroke Castle stood firm against the King, greatly influencing the direction of the war in South Wales. Toward the end of the war, however, in 1648, Major General Laugharne and Colonel Pyer refused to disband their forces causing Laugharne to be imprisoned and Poyer to fortify town and castle for the King, rekindling in the process the dying spark of the Royalist cause throughout South Wales. Adherents to the cause came from all over the Kingdom until, eventually, Oliver Cromwell drew up an army before Pembroke and began a siege which was to last forty-nine days, the defenders of Pembroke receiving no assistance from the Royalist Party.

Following the capture of Pembroke, Cromwell ordered the castle's destruction but so strongly was it built that the job was never entirely carried out; an explosion in the Barbican Tower left the walls still standing and lifted the domed roof bodily

without destroying it.

From that time onward, Pembroke Castle remained derelict until 1880, when the late J. R. Cobb of Brecon devoted three years to the building's restoration. In 1929, the castle came into the possession of Major General Sir Ivor Philipps, K.C.B., D.S.O., who continued the work of restoration and, on his death, the castle passed to his daughter, Mrs. Basil Ramsden, who conveyed the castle to trustees appointed by herself and Pembroke Borough Council, the trustees leasing the building to Pembroke Borough Council who now maintain it.

Picton castle.

WISTON

Wiston castle.

No signposts mark the stumpy remains of this castle which, with that at Narberth, was destroyed by Llywelyn ap Iorwerth in his bid to free Pembrokeshire from the oppressive rule of the Norman Earls of Pembroke who held the area by force of arms, using it not only as a base of operations from which to control parts of Southern Ireland, but as a stronghold in defiance of the English King.

Peace was finally negotiated between Llywelyn and Earl William Marshall II, King Henry granting Cardigan and Carmarthen to the Welsh Prince.

TENBY

There are small remains of a castle overlooking St. Catherine's Island. The feature, however, is the fortified wall enclosing the Old Town area.

Arches have been knocked through the wall's Towers to provide access for motor vehicles and these, one suspects, have been left rough and rugged looking for the benefit of tourists.

Tenby Town Wall.

329

THE END.

FINEM RESPICE.

INDEX